STOIC CLIMBING

2021 Juan Marbarro ©
Translation: Carmen Lozano
Cover design: Gloria Jiménez

Climbing Letters
climbingletters.com

ISBN: 978-84-123960-0-3

STOIC CLIMBING

FINDING WISDOM ON THE ROCK

Juan Marbarro

Contents

Introduction

Why do we climb? What for? Anyone who climbs will have a hard time answering these questions if they haven't thought about them first. There are many reasons for doing so. Everyone can have their own personal reasons, although it is true that from the outside it can be perceived as a useless activity, too risky and meaningless. Climbing to the top and then having to come down later? If you want to get in shape, why don't you go to the gym? —they'll say. But whoever gets on the rock, tries it and learns to enjoy it, knows that it is much more than a physical activity. Challenge, exploration, adventure, nature or a sense of community may be some of the reasons. And yet, the list is endless. It is probably the combination of all of them that creates a powerful synergy. But I think there is still something beyond that. I really believe it has a close connection to the essence of life. And this is what I want to explore over the next few pages.

The purpose of this book is to improve the reader's life through climbing. Climbing is conceived as a tool for growth, a vehicle by which to apply a philosophy of life such as yoga, martial arts, or meditation, whether you are a casual or advanced practitioner.

Every time I go to the rock, despite the physical and mental effort involved, I feel satisfied. Satisfaction levels that are hard to explain. More than any other activity or way of spending my time.

When I climb I feel good, in balance -literally and metaphorically-. Moreover, I bring part of that well-being with me when I return to my daily life. It seems to me that climbing develops tools that allow us to deal with different emotions and situations that arise in life. When we push our own limits we always evolve, and that evolution makes us better in all aspects of life.

Conscious and reflective climbing can become a form of self-knowledge, a journey into your inner self, into unconscious mechanisms and patterns. It is in ascending the mountain that we learn to transcend ourselves.

This book is not intended to make you a better climber or to help you increase a grade. Here you will find some tips to improve your life through climbing. However, if you apply the principles you will find throughout the book, climbing better will be an inevitable consequence.

Everything in our lives is interconnected. No part of ourselves is autonomous or develops outside of our system —physical, mental, emotional. Every decision we make on the rock, every choice, every thought, every attitude, constitutes us. For this reason, I believe that through climbing we can put into practice a series of techniques and tools that can lead us to a better life. At least one in which we can be at peace with ourselves, being able to deal efficiently with the tensions that are generated in everyday life.

We are the result of the combination of everything we live. Every action counts. Every reflection, every experience. Climbing is a good place to cultivate our abilities: the difficulties we encounter on the wall forge our character. Every challenge we overcome nourishes us. Every person we meet teaches us something new. In short, every experience we live in the mountains enriches our lives to unsuspected levels, as we will discover throughout this book.

Just as anyone can benefit from the practice of yoga, meditation or martial arts, anyone can benefit from the practice of climbing whatever their level and degree of involvement. Obviously, the greater the involvement, the greater the results, but there are always positive effects, even in the smallest practice. It is not necessary to have big muscles, nor to climb more grades, nor to dedicate a lot of time to it. Whatever our degree of commitment to the activity, it is simply a matter of trying to live better thanks to the benefits it brings us. Each one at their own pace, and if it goes well, increasing as much as possible.

However, it is important to clarify that here you will not find easy solutions, nor a system or training method, but an attitude, a philosophy of life, an operating system, a framework in which to develop. A laboratory in which to experiment. A template where we can gather experiences that we can then apply to our everyday life. And it is not enough to read: you have to put it into practice, otherwise it becomes mere entertainment. And if you discover that this way of living is interesting for you, you can go as deep as you want, both in theory and in practice.

What is living well?

To live better, you need to know what it means to live well. What does the good life mean to you? It is a question that almost nobody asks themselves and therefore few people know how to answer, even though, obviously, we all want to live as good as possible. Not having a clear picture in our mind of what the good life looks like, most people wander with no direction chasing what is sold to us from the outside as a good life.

Generally, our society and our immediate environment have presented money, status, comfort or security as symbols of the good life. In a consumer society, purchasing power is the star indicator of the good life. Thus, we spend our lives chasing an ever-increasing number of material things external to ourselves. When we get them, we realize that happiness was not there, or at least not a lasting one that can be enjoyed for a good period of time, but rather we find a temporary and fleeting satisfaction. This concept of happiness is designed so we are never content, never satisfied, so we always need more, regardless of what we have achieved and thus be a good consumer and keep moving the economy.

What I would like to cover in this book is to be

subjectively happier. To have a good life from within. Qualitatively, not quantitatively. That is, to feel good. And that is not to accumulate a quantity of things that we thought we should have, but to have emotions that provide us with a positive life experience, from our subjectivity. In contrast, they make us believe that a good life is to collect amounts of things to be happy: like 'X' amount of money in the bank or per month, titles, a car, the latest smartphone or clothes of a certain brand... keeping us submerged in a deep chronic dissatisfaction.

And what is the opposite of continually chasing things and chronic dissatisfaction? Peace of mind, serenity. Something easy to understand, but difficult to achieve. Because to achieve this peace, ironically, you have to use strength. Mental strength. Strength to dominate our mind, to keep it away from the negative emotions that cloud our experience. Strength to encourage positive attitudes such as joy, optimism and the courage to live. Even in the face of the worst conditions, maintaining peace of mind is vital to overcome difficulty, and to do so with as little suffering as possible.

Strength to be able to enjoy everything, to get the best out of every experience, without the need for it to be the most expensive or the most difficult to obtain, such as traveling to a faraway place or owning the most recent model of the latest technological gadget. I'm not saying that it's wrong to consume and do those kinds of things from time to time, but we shouldn't delegate all our happiness to these things. We can also be happy when we don't have them. We can be happy with the simple things; with the things we already own or are close by. The mind tends to forget these things quickly to chase others all the time, causing always high doses of dissatisfaction in the present moment, the only one in which you are and will always be.

Thanks to mental strength we can concentrate on the search for serenity, peace with oneself, good emotional management, and so on. Without letting ourselves be dragged by false providers of instant satisfaction. For this we have to reflect deeply on what we want to identify what is really good for us and what is simply momentarily comforting our insatiable appetite.

Through climbing we can exercise our mental strength and also experience full satisfaction. The serenity derived from accomplishing a project, from overcoming oneself, from effort and its results, from self-knowledge, from breaking our limits or accepting things as they are.

If the goal of our life is to consume and seek security, why is it so satisfying to climb a mountain or simply walk in nature? Doing the activity, living the experience, exploring, sharing, spending time outdoors are things that bring so much more than buying the "necessary" shoes or equipment to do it.

Don't get it twisted.

In my attempt to understand why the practice of climbing is so beneficial I have spent several years reflecting and comparing climbing with other disciplines or philosophies, finding parallels between the practice of climbing and some of these based primarily on self-improvement. From here, I turned the tables. Instead of trying to understand climbing through other disciplines, I focused on trying to understand life through climbing. Analyzing every situation, every sensation, every experience I had climbing and extrapolating it to other life situations, also looking for similarities with other philosophies and ways of experiencing to identify the patterns that lead us to feel this crazy love for climbing walls that lead nowhere.

Immersed in this search, I found an ancient philosophy, born in Greece about two thousand three hundred years ago that, from my point of view, is similar to the values of climbing and, moreover, complements it, that is, this philosophy applies very well to the field of climbing and climbing is improved with the application of this philosophy.

It is Stoicism, a particularly practical philosophy, which despite being so ancient is still widely studied and practiced around the world today, even giving a resurgence of this in recent years in which the frequent changes and uncertainty leave us more exposed than ever.

Why Stoicism?

Stoicism is a practical philosophy, for the real world. A doctrine that has been developed throughout its long history, not to be a set of theories and reflections on existence, but a practical guide to achieve peace of mind, and therefore, a better life.

In the Stoic texts we speak rather of the concept of virtue, which translated to our time would come to mean strength of character, peace of mind, courage, wisdom and self-discipline. Since the term "virtue" is not easy to translate in our current language, its meaning is somewhat abstract. That is why we will always use instead some of the qualities that are part of the set of meanings of virtue, such as serenity, wisdom or mental strength, to give some examples.

The Stoics thought that the only way to have a good life was to have a virtuous life, or, in other words, to have the qualities described above, such as peace of mind or strength of character. By peace of mind (virtue), they understood the reduction of negative emotions, giving priority to positive ones, such as joy and happiness. To this end, they developed techniques and tools with which to deal with negative emotions such as anger, sadness, anxiety or fear, and thus reduce their impact on life.

Stoicism emerged in Greece around 300 B.C. Zeno of Citium was a merchant who arrived in Athens ruined after a shipwreck and studied philosophy until he founded his own school. He did not give his lessons in closed classes, but in the open air, under the porches (stoa) of the city streets so that it was accessible to anyone who wanted to listen. Since then, it has been evolving and being interpreted with the same purpose: to provide serenity and peace of mind to whoever is interested in achieving it.

It reached its maximum splendor in ancient Rome, where there were great Stoic references such as Epictetus —who went from being a slave to directing his own philosophical school—, Seneca (senator and writer) or Marcus Aurelius (Roman emperor). These three Stoics will be widely quoted throughout this analysis of Stoicism through climbing, since they have contributed several of the clearest and most practical texts on Stoicism —of those that are still preserved—. And furthermore, we can benefit from it in different aspects of life.

Since Stoicism and its tools have a practical approach, it is not enough to just read about it, it must be implemented and practiced if we want to obtain any kind of benefit. Theory without practice is just words and ideas floating around. With this premise, we want to use climbing to practice stoicism. Just as chess improves cognitive abilities, stimulating strategic thinking and creativity, climbing can improve our stoic abilities, which in turn will improve our life by providing us with serenity, peace of mind and strength of character.

By strength of character I mean the strength that will be necessary to manage our emotions so that we do not allow ourselves to be dragged down by the negative ones that disturb our peace and happiness. Just as we use a certain hold or a certain training to improve a certain grip that we will later need on the rock, we can use climbing to improve skills —mental strength, emotional management, serenity— that we can then use in life. Just as we train our physical strength at home or in a climbing wall to then go to the rock to achieve the goals we have set for ourselves, we climb to stimulate our mental strength and then take advantage of it in every circumstance that life throws at us.

It's like when the doctor recommends swimming to strengthen your back to alleviate aches and pains. There is an intention. Sure, you may enjoy the idea of taking some time out to swim and get physically fit, but deep down you have a greater goal. You are looking for a specific benefit that will affect your quality of life; in this case, to be free of back discomfort. So, I propose we enjoy climbing as we have always done, and then use it as well as a mean to achieve a greater goal such as living better, more serene. With more wisdom. Practical wisdom. Giving more intentionality to our climbs, making them more consciously and getting the most out of every moment.

Therefore, I encourage you take everything that seems practical and interesting about stoicism and implement it consciously when you are in the middle of a big rock. If, thanks to these techniques, you are able to successfully manage the emotions that arise when climbing, you will be able to extrapolate and apply them in any other situation in your life.

This book is intended as an introduction to stoicism, and thus we only approach some of the concepts that I consider most useful and practical, so that they are easily applicable to climbing and daily life. When you put them into practice and observe how beneficial this vital attitude can be, you will probably want to go deeper into this philosophy, which even today is still being studied, reinterpreted and adapted to the changing times we live in.

Nowadays, it is easy to get in touch with online communities dedicated to studying and discussing Stoicism. In fact, in recent years, there is resurgence in the adoption of this philosophy that provides practical tools for dealing with life in these uncertain times of economic crises, pandemics, disruptive technologies, new political movements, over-information, fake news and the list could go on.

Stoicism is and has been practiced by leaders of all kinds; emperors, politicians, businessmen, artists, athletes, etcetera. Anyone can benefit from it, but people who have a great deal of responsibility and are used to dealing with all kinds of obstacles and difficulties in their daily lives find it especially useful. It is designed to achieve happiness and wisdom, to be more resilient to the onslaughts of life, to gain freedom from events outside ourselves, to not let ourselves be carried away by excessive comforts and, ultimately and as a consequence of all of the above, to be better people. The best version of ourselves.

In my opinion, climbers can benefit greatly from stoic techniques given the nature of our activity. In climbing we must deal with obstacles, difficulties, unforeseen events or emotions such as frustration and fear. We must apply a great amount of will and mental strength to carry our body against gravity along a wall. And, if in addition to applying stoicism to our climbing, we can take some lessons home from the mountain, all the better.

Why climbing?

Climbing brings out a multitude of emotions. Rock has the power to amplify them to another level. It is a catalyst of experiences: fear feels more intense when you are hanging several meters high. The same with anxiety, frustration or anger. Or joy, satisfaction and happiness.

The person who climbs has to deal with himself and with the environment —the rock, the weather conditions or the people, among other things— in their practice. This is why I consider climbing an ideal laboratory for applying stoic wisdom into practice. The aim of this book is, through climbing, to lay the foundations and mental schemes necessary to implement and transfer stoicism and its benefits to any aspect of life. I am not going to propose a method. Nor specific techniques. Rather, I want to reflect on some tools that can be of great practical use throughout the exercise of climbing and that will also provide us with new perspectives on life in general.

Just as a Buddhist practices meditation several hours a day to obtain a peace of mind that will be useful throughout their existence, the climber can consciously use the practice of climbing to obtain benefits that will extend to all areas of their life (for example, the control of negative emotions). In fact, I consider climbing as a form of meditation. A more Western form of meditation than Zen or yoga, but essentially the same: concentration and mastery of attention in order to achieve serenity and be present in the moment.

It is more difficult to concentrate meditating sitting on the floor or maintaining a series of static stretches in which every last muscle aches, than progressing vertically on a rock. And the main difference is that on the rock you have no choice but to be concentrated. The moment you lose focus or your thoughts go beyond what is in front of you, there is a high probability that you will fail and have to regain your concentration if you want to get to the top. Climbing is eminently practical and has a clear purpose, in contrast to a meditation in which the final goal is to empty the mind, something extremely difficult for our wild and overloaded mind.

Climbing can be said to provide the necessary focus to carry out a personal transformation. This practice can be done at all levels. From beginners to professionals. From occasional or weekend practitioners, to those who live in their van in front of the mountain. Everyone can benefit to a greater or lesser extent from the practice of stoicism through climbing. Just as practicing any sport will improve your health and well-being, even if you never get to compete. In climbing you are only competing against yourself.

Although we sometimes tend to compare ourselves, the challenge is always against ourselves and how we manage our abilities and emotions to achieve what we intend to do.

Since climbing is about breaking limits, increasing our tolerance for risk or becoming comfortable in discomfort, let's take all that effort and transform it into our medicine for everyday life. Let's consciously pick up the lessons experienced on the wall and learn to live better.

Life is full of challenges and the way we face and manage them shapes everything. Just as when we climb, we consider discomfort as a challenge, an adventure, a quest to overcome; in life we could have a similar attitude, a stoic attitude that allows us to always find the best sequences or the best holds to continue upwards.

For the examples and metaphors, I have chosen to focus on rock climbing in its most sporty modality, specifically on the concepts of free climbing —not to be confused with free solo—, understood as climbing that has the aim of reaching the top, using the protection material such as the rope and the prefixed anchors, but without resting by hanging on to the anchor or falling on the way up (what is known as sending a route). This type of climbing is not only one of the most accessible for those who want to start, but it is also the most practiced around the world. While some of the techniques and reflections

I propose could be applied to other types of climbing such as traditional, bouldering, competition, big wall, or alpinism, I wanted to express myself on a common ground for the majority of the community. However you choose to challenge yourself, you will certainly be able to adapt the ideas you find in this book to your personal practice.

In addition, I would like to give it a greater meaning than just a sport or leisure practice. Climbing provides opportunities for growth, for the development of positive and beneficial qualities for our lives such as mental strength, courage, hard work, humility, concentration or even gratitude. All of these are also qualities of great value in Stoic philosophy. That is why I speak of stoic climbing.

Practicing discomfort

Much has been said in recent years about the importance of stepping out of the comfort zone and breaking our limitations. This is something that the Stoics already practiced a very long time ago and in a very particular, simple and easy to apply way. The Stoics voluntarily exercised discomfort in various ways, such as wearing light clothing when it was cold, going a little hungry and thirsty from time to time, eating simple food, sleeping on the floor, or showing up to a social event wearing clothes that were "different" from the established norm. Although it might seem that they wanted to suffer on purpose, they actually gained great benefits from it, such as losing the fear of suffering discomfort in the future, exercising mental strength or learning to appreciate the simple things.

Climbing itself is an exercise of discomfort. Who would rather suffer in the middle of a mountain than enjoy the scenery from below over a beer? Climbing throws you straight out of your physical and mental comfort zone. It is an exercise of will. Of mental strength. To fight, individually and with as little material as possible, against the force of gravity. Against our most inherent fear: the fear of falling. Gravity attracts us and forces us to be as close to the ground as possible, it is not a whim. So any attempt to get off the ground against this force is an act that requires great willpower, a strong and clear intention.

Willpower is something that can be trained. The more you exercise it, the more you have it. It is one of the main characteristics of mental strength and can be used for many things: from climbing a mountain to finishing any project. Or to start a new one. To abandon bad habits and create better ones, to fight for what is considered right, or for a purpose. To leave places where we don't feel good and explore new possibilities.

Almost everything we want to achieve in life involves discomfort, and we will need large doses of willpower to achieve it. It is never easy, even knowing that the rewards will be great. Willpower is a tool that can be sharpened. The Stoics knew this and consciously sharpened it. Climbers do it too, more or less consciously, but we do it.

There are many examples of this exercise of will through discomfort in climbing. When we have a choice between leading a route or going top-rope and we choose to do it leading, we are voluntarily exercising discomfort —the physical difficulty of the route is the same, but psychologically it is more difficult/uncomfortable if you carry the rope under your feet when you lead than when you have it overhead when you go top-rope—. In this way, we are exercising our mental strength by increasing the perceived risk and difficulty of the climb itself. Practicing falls to lose the fear of falling is another example of how we practice discomfort to expand our chances of climbing successfully.

The physical effort of any sport training, be it walking, biking, mountain climbing, etc., strengthens the body, just as the difficulties —facing challenges of daily life, problem solving, tackling mountains...— strengthen the mind. It prepares us for the possible discomforts we are likely to experience in our lives. To lose fear of them, to exchange anxiety about the future for full confidence in our ability to adapt to any situation. The Stoics practiced poverty in order to not fear it and to be ready if by any misfortune we had to face it. When you have voluntarily gone hungry and cold and you see that it is no big deal, you lose the fear of it happening again for some reason.

> "The art of living is more like wrestling than dancing, in so far as it stands ready against the accidental and the unforeseen, and is not apt to fall."
>
> Marcus Aurelius[1]

When you've learned that falling trying a route doesn't look so serious or dangerous, you are free to go all out, without restraint and without fear of falling unexpectedly. This exercise in discomfort is even more effective when it is done directed toward our fears and weaknesses. Afraid of falling? Fall.

[1] Meditations, Book VII, 61, transl. Ramón Bach Pellicer

Don't like slab climbing? Go do it as many times as you can. Fear of loneliness? Spend time alone. Fear of not having or losing money? Live on less. And so on with anything you can think of —and especially with the ones that limit you the most—. It's better to face difficulties and grow because of them than to always choose the easy path and remain stagnant.

> "Set aside a certain number of days, during which you shall be content with the scantiest and cheapest fare, with coarse and rough dress, saying to yourself the while: "Is this the condition that I feared?"
>
> Seneca[2]

The conscious practice of discomfort expands our comfort zone, our ability to feel comfortable in a wider range of situations. We lose our fear of discomfort. And, therefore, we are freer.

We are freer because we have the ability to function better in a wider range of situations and we are not conditioned by our attachment to comfort. As we climb, we progress in our strength (physical and mental) and our technique, we gain confidence and, therefore, access to more possibilities. We can start climbing different types of routes, on different types of rock and levels. Arriving at a new climbing area and choosing between several projects without having to stick to a few routes where we feel comfortable, that gives you freedom.

---

[2] Moral Letters to Lucilius, Book XVIII, Transl. Richard M. Gummere

When there's no room in the shelter and you don't mind sleeping on the mountain sacrificing comfort, that's freedom. It gives you lightness, not carrying the burden of the need for pleasure and comfort. You can be just as happy eating rice at the foot of the mountain as you are tasting dishes in the best restaurant. You will not base your decisions on the amount of comfort or pleasure available. You will choose the routes you really want to do, not the easiest or most popular. Not the ones that allow you to sleep a little longer or have the best access.

> "He who pursues pleasure postpones everything to it, disregards that first essential, liberty, and sacrifices it to his belly; nor does he buy pleasure for himself, but sells himself to pleasure."
>
> Seneca[3]

It is also a reflective exercise. Of learning to discern between what we really need and what we don't, between what is important and what is secondary. Reevaluating priorities. A weekend climbing in the mountains can be uncomfortable, it's hot or cold, you're going to get dirty, there are insects everywhere, you're going to eat simple food, you're going to sleep badly in a tent and your muscles are going to ache the days after. But you will also feel great satisfaction from doing what you love to do, pushing your limits, leaving the comfort of the couch and

---

[3] On happiness, chapter XIV

the movies behind and going out to live your life, to create your own story. It is important to spend time resting in comfort when we need it, but it should not be a priority, a vital routine. Life is in the discomfort and in applying our will to expand our limits.

Another "side effect" of practicing discomfort (whether with climbing or any other technique) is that you will be more grateful. More humble and more easily happy. Practice discomfort to enjoy comfort easier. When you eat when you are hungry, drink water when you are thirsty, or go to sleep when you are tired. What great and simple pleasures! Descending a route after fighting for it, trying and failing several times and finally succeeding. To look down from below to contemplate with satisfaction and be grateful for the opportunity to enjoy this experience, the nature, the landscape and the good company.

Perception

Perceptions are the way we interpret the impressions received from the outside to form an idea of reality. Our perceptions are often largely biased by our emotions.

What makes us like to repeat some routes and not others? Why do some people hate one type of climbing and others love it? Generally, when we form our opinion there are underlying emotions associated with it and that creates an appreciation or dislike. If one day I climb a project and send it on the first try, I will probably like that route forever. Not to mention other factors such as being highly motivated that day, having good environmental conditions as well as being physically and mentally strong. However, if I arrive at another similar route (or even the same one) tired, after climbing other routes, on a very hot day... I will probably fail. And I will create a negative perception of that route. It will seem difficult, laborious, not flowing enough.

Our perception often depends on our experience. If we are used to walking quite a bit in our day-to-day lives or traveling long distances in the mountains, our perception of what is far to walk to will be different from that of someone who drives to the gym or to buy bread. The distance is the same, but the perception is different.

The way we judge external reality is not as objective as it should be. If you encounter a type of grip that you don't have much experience with or have had negative experiences with in the past, it's possible that the negative emotions that come with facing that step are increasing the difficulty for no real reason. Something external —the grip judged as "bad"— is triggering an internal negative response in you. If you fail several times attempting the project, it is an external event as well. It's something that's happening outside. The frustration and anger you are feeling is an internal process.

The Stoics advocated that through reason we can analyze impressions and the emotions they trigger in order to have a clearer perception. Even transforming our perception from something negative to something positive or neutral. Complaining and reacting negatively rarely serves any purpose other than to add more suffering to any event. We have the ability to think rationally to transform our perceptions.

> "If you are pained by any external thing, it is not this thing that disturbs you, but your own judgement about it. And it is in your power to wipe out this judgement now."
>
> Marcus Aurelius[4]

---

[4] Meditations, Book VIII, 47. Transl. George Long

Be objective

"Don't let the force of an impression when it first hits you knock you off your feet; just say to it, "Hold on a moment; let me see who you are and what you represent. Let me put you to the test."

Epictetus[5]

As we have seen, our impressions are charged with emotions that influence the perception of reality. Moreover, we tend to believe that reality is as we perceive it, disregarding this emotional part we are talking about.

In climbing we can see a clear example of this bias. The routes are always the same, the rock does not change. They are the most objective and inert thing that exists. A piece of rock in the middle of a mountain, just like that, as simple as that. What changes are our perceptions of it. The subjectivity we apply to it. An experienced climber would perceive a route as easy, while a beginner would see it as impossible. Or if you climb a route of your grade on top rope, it will be much easier than if you do it leading. The rock is the same, the only thing that changes is your perception.

---

[5] Discourses and selected writings. Transl. Robert Dobbin

The concept of grade[6] itself is very subjective. You could say it is a shared subjectivity. The climbing community evaluates a route based on the perceived difficulty and comparing it to their experience on other routes. Although this system is well established, this does not mean it is a universal truth. New techniques or new protection materials can change the grade of a route, as is currently being discussed with the issue of the use of knee pads. It is also possible that a route has a medium or easy grade but the steps are difficult to read because of the rock formations. Too many variables influence our subjectivity —and that of others—. How many times have you discussed over beers whether a route has a very difficult pitch for its grade or whether it seemed too easy or whether a "letter" should be added to the number, or removed! But it's all part of our perceptions, the ideas we form after subjectively filtering information.

Likewise, if you top-rope, that same route would be much easier than if you lead. The rock is the same, the steps are exactly the same, the movements are the same, the only thing that changes is your perception.

You're about to clip. You just put the quickdraw on. One foot resting on a tiny rock ledge and the other on grip. Your left hand keeps your body glued to the wall thanks to a couple of centimeters at the right angle where you can fit three fingers. You go to grab the rope to clip and realize how far away the

---

[6] See "climbing grades" in the glossary (page 114)

previous bolt is. Your whole body tenses up, you're starting to get tired, you have to act! You grab the rope and slowly pull it to the carabiner on the quick-draw and clip it through easily. You are now clipped in. The tension is released. And now you realize that you were in a much more comfortable position than you thought, so much so that you even enjoy talking to your belayer or dipping your hands into the chalk bag to get some rest before continuing.

What was the difference before and after clipping? The rock was the same, the grip and position were the same. The climber's perception was making the difference, making it all the more difficult when there was more perceived risk. It doesn't even make sense, but that's how we operate.

> "Our lack of confidence is not the result of difficulty. The difficulty comes from our lack of confidence."
>
> Seneca[7]

Observe and analyze objectively, without judging, without thinking or classifying between easy-difficult or good-bad. Just it is what it is.

When we contemplate a new project, we tend to make a series of judgments that, in most cases, do not help us achieve our objective. We judge the route first based on the grade other climbers have given to it. This is a good way to orient ourselves, but it is still a subjective evaluation of others, as I have just

---

[7] Moral Letters to Lucilius, Letter CIV. Transl. Richard M. Gummere

said. Then our impressions are influenced by our own assessment of the types of holds we have, the distance between bolts, if someone failed or sent the route before me, if I'm tired today, if my climbing shoes are worn out, and so on. And it goes on, each of us with our own favorite mental story. Instead, just observe: type of rock, type of grip, possible sequences, analyze different possibilities. Try to make it as clear as possible, without clouding reality with your subjectivity. Without involving past frustrations and insecurities in your analysis.

Surely you have heard (or said) the phrase: "There is nothing, I can't find any holds". This would be objectively false, because if the route is bolted and is often repeated by other people it is because there is something. Then it would be better to say: "I can't grab anything from my position" or "I am not in a position to grab anything around me". In this way we will be speaking clearly and we will be closer to finding the solution, either by moving our feet, resting or taking perspective of the situation. By transforming our speech into a more objective one, we open up more possibilities for action.

Taking perspective is a good practice. Sometimes we get confused trying to do something and without realizing it, we are loading a simple crack in a rock with subjectivity. From trying so hard to hold it — probably from the wrong position— it becomes more and more difficult to do so and we fall sooner. Our subjectivity, that is, simply thinking that it is difficult or that we may fall, predisposes our body to fall, tending to bend our legs and leave our hips down.

In these moments, is a very good idea to take a step back, distance ourselves to clear our mind and our perception. Also, very productive since you will rest, and so, you will achieve your goal sooner. Maybe even take some deep breaths to help you recover that mental balance, calm your mind and emotions. Once relaxed, clearly visualize reality and its possibilities.

A good exercise in taking perspective and removing our subjective baggage from a wall is to analyze the route as if you were describing it to another climber who is currently climbing much higher grades than you. You wouldn't tell someone who climbs really hard that a two-finger pocket hold is uncomfortable, you would simply tell them that there's a two-finger pocket and then there's a crimp and a foot hole.

In fact, communicating with other people on the mountain is a great exercise in precision and objectivity. When you describe a difficult step to someone who is struggling in the middle of the wall you have to be as precise as possible. You could say: "get a good hold over there on the left" on a crack-filled wall. But it would be more effective to say: "grab an inch-deep crimp by fully stretching your left arm diagonally". In the first sentence "good" is something totally subjective, what is good for the sender may not be so good for the receiver-climber and may confuse them.

Focus on what's important. On the basics. Look at the rock as it is and yourself as you are. As a piece of rock with some cracks and holes to place your hands and feet. Don't think about whether or not you send this route or the other. Whether the route is more or less popular in the local crag. Whether you get it before your partner or not. Whether the equipment you use is of one brand or another, whether your climbing shoes are the most expensive or the cheapest. You don't need to have the most expensive gear or the brand that spends the most on marketing to be better at climbing. Recognize what has real value. What really has value to you. The experience, the company, the satisfaction of improving yourself or the wisdom you gain from each situation are the things that are truly valuable in climbing, above ticking off routes or having the best gear —always keeping safety in mind, not walking around with poor quality or worn out gear that compromises your physical integrity—. Sometimes, we are so contaminated by our own and other people's emotions —such as what others think or the marketing we are exposed to— that we don't even know that they are conditioning us, so we must make a conscious effort to dismantle the emotional layers that cover everything we perceive.

"Like seeing roasted meat and other dishes in front of you and suddenly realizing: This is a dead fish. A dead bird. A dead pig. Or that this noble vintage is grape juice, and the purple robes are sheep wool dyed with shellfish blood."

Marcus Aurelius[8]

---

[8] Meditations, Book VI, 13. Transl. Gregory Hays

Acceptance

Once you have been able to see things as they are, analyzing (and dismantling if necessary) your impressions, it is time to accept. Accepting things as they are and not thinking about how we would like them to be. Not even for a second.

You're climbing and you're going up little by little until you encounter a step that is more complicated than you thought it would be. You want to face it objectively, rationally. You hold the grip and move your feet to start the sequence. You try to move the other hand and bam, you fall. "What a bad grip, the friction of the rock is bad, it looked easier and now I don't know if I can do it!". These statements are related to unrealistic expectations. Things that only exist in our mind. As you know very well, the crimp or the edge that you have to hold on to in order to overcome the step is not going to change, it is a piece of rock that has been there for thousands of years, so it won't turn now into whatever you want it to be. The sooner you accept things as they are, the sooner you can take action and find a way to overcome the obstacle, and the less time and energy you will waste.

"Remember: you shouldn't be surprised that a fig tree

produces figs, nor the world what it produces. A good doctor isn't surprised when his patients have fever, or a helmsman when the wind blows against him."

Marcus Aurelius[9]

Life is what it is. The route is what it is. Your strengths are what they are. You are where you are and you can only be here and now. Don't get attached to your expectations. Maybe you thought it was your time to get that project you've been chasing for so long, or that you'd get a new job, or get a better grade on a test. Maybe you thought the weather would be nice when you were traveling. Or you probably find yourself struggling in the middle of a route that you judged to be easier than it really is. And, in the end, it all didn't turn out the way you expected. But don't get attached. External things cannot be changed. They are the way they are, and you must take them as they come. As Epictetus said, "don't wish for figs in winter." It seems that the Stoics were very fond of figs.

"If you long for your son or your friend, when it is not given you to have him, know that you are longing for a fig in winter time. For as winter is to the fig, so is the whole pressure of the universe to that which it destroys".

Epictetus[10]

Just enjoy them in the summer and in the winter

---

[9] Meditations, Book VII, 15. Transl. Gregory Hays
[10] Disertaciones por Arriano, Book III, XXIV, 87. Transl. Paloma Ortiz García

something else will come along. Maybe even your plans were cancelled due to unforeseen circumstances or you got injured, but there is no need to ruminate about what you are missing or what you would like to be doing. There are no figs now, but there will be in the future. There may only be almonds now, they're not as sweet, but you can enjoy them in their own way too. There is always something you can do.

> "The cucumber is bitter? Then throw it out. There are brambles in the path? Then go around them. That's all you need to know. Nothing more. Don't demand to know "why such things exist." Anyone who understands the world will laugh at you, just as a carpenter would if you seemed shocked at finding sawdust in his workshop, or a shoemaker at scraps of leather left over from work".
>
> Marcus Aurelius[11]

Every time you set your mind to something, especially if it is something external to you, you are exposed to the risk that it will not turn out the way you want it to. Accepting this from the beginning will save you a lot of frustration in the future. This does not mean that you should not fight for it with all your effort, being aware of where you have more capacity to influence so you don't waste your strength.

As you can already guess, and we will look into it further later on, the only things we can be able to manage are our thoughts and our actions. Observe

[11] Meditations, Book VIII, 50. Transl. Gregory Hays

objectively and surrender to the situation, to the present moment. And regain confidence in yourself, in your ability to adapt, to give an effective response to the challenges you face.

> "Floods will rob us of one thing, fire of another. These are conditions of our existence which we cannot change. What we can do is adopt a noble spirit, such a spirit as befits a good man, so that we may bear up bravely under all that fortune sends us and bring our wills into tune with nature's."
>
> Seneca[12]

Like the Buddhists, the Stoics considered that the root of suffering lies in desire. Continually desiring things that we don't have or that don't exist. However, while the Buddhists advocate the complete dissolution of desire, to desire nothing and thus not to suffer, the Stoics advocated desiring what one already has, what already is, the way it is.

> "Don't seek to have events happen as you wish, but wish them to happen as they do happen, and all will be well with you."
>
> Epictetus[13]

---

[12] Letters from a Stoic, Letter CVII. Transl. Robin Campbell ˙
[13] The Enchiridion, 8. Transl. Margarita Mosquera

Amor Fati

Love your destiny. And by destiny I mean everything that happens to you. Welcome everything that comes your way. Sometimes things do not go as we expect, but this is not necessarily negative. As I have already said, besides accepting things as they are, we will do better if we also "love" them as they are, learning to appreciate them. All things have their good and bad sides. There are things that, although they may seem negative at a certain moment, may have positive consequences in the long run, even though we may not be able to see them right now. Moreover, they probably even have something positive in the present, even though it is very difficult to see at first glance.

If while climbing a wall you come across a slab —which you insist you are not good at— you have two options. Either you can grumble and grudgingly do it, suffering and probably expending more energy than necessary and probably falling, or you can accept it willingly, take it as a learning experience and find ways to enjoy the process. Also, working on that weakness will lead you to be a more complete climber and be more resourceful in future similar situations.

Rock is like life. It puts situations in front of you

that you have to deal with if you want to reach your goals. You must choose how to take those situations, whether as something to suffer or as something to enjoy, love and be grateful for. Which attitude do you think will be more bearable? Which one will lead you more easily to success?

Because, at the end of the day, why waste energy thinking about how you would like it to be? Why waste your life wishing for something to be different? The past cannot be changed and the present is what it is. Live in the present, which is the only thing that exists at this moment. One hand, one foot, another hand, clip, visualize, another foot... and climb on. What's the point of complaining? Okay, you almost had it, you missed the dumbest step. You can take it as a learning experience. Learn to never relax too soon. To stay alert until the end. A lesson you learn now will save you from repeating mistakes in the future. And appreciating what has happened to you now for what it is, a lesson, saves you suffering in the present as well. Complaining rarely serves any purpose other than to waste energy we could be using to resolve the problem at hand.

Were you turned down on a job interview? Rather take this as an opportunity to improve your presentation, a practice on how to handle this kind of situations so that you will have a better chance next time when you apply for an even better position. Do you think you made a bad decision? You can't know. Every decision, every path we take leads us to different possibilities. Some you may judge as good and some as bad, but not everything is good and not everything is bad. So it's better to focus on the good parts of each situation —there's always a silver lining— even if sometimes it takes more effort to find them. Let's say you're pretty confident and you think you can climb a certain grade or even a big wall. But you're trying similar routes and you're not doing well. You can't make progress, you can't clip or you fall more than you'd like. Instead of getting frustrated and complaining about your current abilities you can reflect on what you need to improve and even be grateful for the fact that, by realizing your true abilities now, you have saved yourself a lot of future suffering by trying to tackle harder climbs without being sufficiently prepared to tackle them. A dose of humility, which doesn't have to be a negative thing. Don't reject anything, take it as it comes and try to focus on the part that is more bearable for you.

> "Everything has two handles: one by which it may be borne, another by which it cannot. If your brother acts unjustly, do not lay hold on the affair by the handle of his injustice, for by that it cannot be borne, but rather by the opposite —that he is your brother, that he was brought up with you; and thus you will lay hold on it as it is to be borne."
>
> Epictetus[14]

[14] The Enchiridion, 43. Transl. Margarita Mosquera

Try to bring attention to the good side of things, to their benefit, and just ignore the negative side. Is your favorite climbing spot a bit overcrowded? You can take it by its uncomfortable handle, its negative side, such as having to wait to climb a route or the deterioration on the rock. Or you can take it on the plus side, as a chance to meet new people and connect more with the community. Or that there's more likelihood of new routes opening up, or finding new people to enjoy climbing with. You decide which way you take it.

> "Accept the things to which fate binds you, and love the people with whom fate brings you together, but do so with all your heart."
>
> Marcus Aurelius[15]

Why do things happen if not to make us evolve? Why do you get into climbing a route of increasing higher grade? Besides practicing discomfort as we advanced at the beginning of the book, we seek to improve ourselves and grow.

> "True happiness is to enjoy the present, without anxious dependence upon the future, not to amuse ourselves with either hopes or fears but to rest satisfied with what we have, which is sufficient."
>
> Seneca[16]

---

[15] Meditations, Book VI, 39
[16] The Morals of Seneca: A Selection of his Prose, Chapter I. Trans Walter Clode

It sounds a bit fatalistic to talk about accepting things as they come. But the thing is there is no other way it can occur. The past is over. The present is happening right now. What is happening right now is the result of an accumulation of things that, although we usually don't know the connection, has its cause in the past. Something like a kind of "karma", as we would popularly say in the West. If I do bad things, bad things will happen to me. If I do good things, good things will happen to me. This is an extremely simplified meaning of the concept of karma itself, but it is the way it commonly tends to be interpreted. A mystical or divine force that rewards or punishes our actions.

But we can understand it in another way, more physical, more based on reason, as a natural law of cause and effect. The problem is that we usually see the effect, but rarely can we discern the cause. Let's look at it with a climbing example:

You're climbing, trying to send a project. You're doing great, but suddenly you miss a hold and fall. Poof! "I almost had it, why did I have to fall just at this moment?" Well, yes, you had to fall, period. It's up to you (literally and figuratively) to learn or keep falling until you learn. If instead of lamenting your fall, you accept reality, embrace it as it is and reflect on the whys and whatnot, you will discover that it could not have been otherwise. A series of circumstances made it quite unlikely that you would make it. Maybe you were tired, or overconfident, maybe the type of grip you had to hold was one you haven't practiced too much, maybe you were more afraid than you needed to be at that moment, and so forth. Then, until you work on all the causes that have provoked this effect, you will continue to have more or less similar results. There is little mysticism in this. In every action there is reward or punishment. If you work on your weaknesses, strive to overcome your fears and look for ways to do things better, you will inevitably achieve what you set out to do.

Therefore, every time we "love our destiny", even though it does not always turn out the way we want it to, we must also reflect and look for the opportunity for growth that it gives us. This way you will be able to get the most out of every situation, without resisting or indulging in false expectations.

Opportunity

Once you see things as they are (objectively), have accepted them and even appreciate that they are as they are, it is time to transform your present into a source of good opportunities. Focus energy on making the most of what you have, without wasting time thinking about how you would like it to be or how it could have been.

> "A blazing fire makes flame and brightness out of everything that is thrown into it."
>
> Marcus Aurelius[17]

Whenever you find yourself dealing with some kind of situation, you can look for ways to transform it into something positive, into something that will make you grow and improve. As I said before, our impressions shape our reality. Making a negative impression of a situation or circumstance will make us try to fight against it and waste all our energy. Instead, we must work on transforming this negative impression into a positive one by seeking opportunity. The way we create opportunity is personal and tailored to each situation.

---

[17] Meditations, Book X, 31. Transl. Gregory Hays

We can recognize opportunity in situations that, at first glance, seem disadvantageous: the opportunity to test yourself, to improve, to practice your peace of mind, or simply the opportunity to try something different.

The opportunity to test yourself happens when you face a difficulty and make use of resources that you either don't usually use or didn't know you had. Remember that the best way to learn something is by practice, by experimenting. You can watch all the videos you want about crack climbing, but won't really learn until you try it. Maybe, thanks to your experience on other holds or in the climbing gym, you internalized some technique, but it won't be until you encounter a crack on a route that you'll have a chance to really put it into practice and test your skills. So, if you find yourself on a route in a crack climbing section, instead of thinking that you've never done it before and that it's difficult, think about the opportunity it grants you, how this situation allows you to test yourself and really see how good you are at it. Thanks to a difficulty, we find the opportunity to improve and our shortcomings become evident to us.

"It is impossible for a man to learn what he thinks he already knows."

Epictetus[18]

It is when our limitations are highlighted that we

---

[18] Discourses, Book II. Chapter XVII

can become aware of the need to improve and take action. When you are climbing and you are faced with a difficult step, and strength starts to abandon you, you can get frustrated by your lack of strength or complain that the step is difficult, but none of this is going to change. However, you can take it as an opportunity to improve by going home and training to increase your strength. Or, if you want an even more instant opportunity, you can try climbing more efficiently, using less energy in tackling the steps previous to the one you find difficult and resting every time the rock allows you to. Thanks to that difficult step, you'll reap benefits —improved strength or improved efficiency— that will make your life easier in the long run, on and off of the rock.

> "The impediment to action advances action. What stands in the way becomes the way."
>
> Marcus Aurelius[19]

We could say that the opportunity to practice your peace of mind is a meta-opportunity. The opportunity of opportunities. It would be the opportunity to put into practice what you are learning in this book. Climbing, although it is a very demanding activity that also involves some risk, is also, as I advanced at the beginning of the book, a wonderful opportunity to exercise our mental strength, as well as our courage and our temperance. In short, our peace of

---

[19] Meditations, Book V, 20. Transl. Gregory Hays

mind. Climbing offers us the opportunity to practice these qualities, which we will benefit from in different aspects of our lives. Becoming more patient, hard-working, better at dealing with difficulties and frustrations, etc. The experiences we live on the rock are a great opportunity to learn to remain calm in the face of all kinds of difficulties, always being more prepared to face the unpredictable situations that life throws at us.

We can also recognize the opportunity to do something different. We tend to learn to do things in a specific way and always repeat these patterns over and over. Our brain likes to create systems to conserve energy. If grabbing the rock using an arm lock-off has worked for us a couple of times, our mind will already create a pattern, a system that it will try to apply to a variety of situations. However, on many occasions these patterns do not work. They are not always the best choice and are often even counterproductive. Climbing locking off with one arm is far from the most efficient.

Climbing teaches us the wide variety of different combinations that can be used to do the same thing. One climber can place their body in a totally different way than another climber on the same route and both end up doing it successfully. Some people do more dynamic movements and others do more static ones. There are only a few situations in which there is only one possible combination to solve the problem. In this way, thanks to a difficulty —a sequence that we can't seem to get right— we find the opportunity to try new things, to try something different from what we usually do and that in this case does not work. Trial and error. Stop doing things just because you've always done them a certain way and experiment with other options that may work for you. In this way you will improve in general, incorporate new resources and tools to your system, and expand your possibilities.

The above are just a few examples of difficulties that are transformed into opportunities. You can find many more ways to recognize the gift hidden behind every circumstance if you reflect on it. Every problem, every difficulty, every failure... Everything brings new opportunities with it. A new motivation, a new way to adapt to the environment.

Don't let negative emotions such as fear or frustration cloud your reality, don't let them hinder your ability to detect the path of opportunity.

In the next chapter we will see how we can direct our action to transform those opportunities into effective success, without wasting our energy.

> "It is in no man's power to have whatever he wants, but he has it in his power not to wish for what he hasn't got, and cheerfully make the most of the things that do come his way."
>
> Seneca[20]

[20] Letters from a Stoic, Letter CXXIII. Transl. Robin Campbell

What depends on me

We have seen that we should accept and even love our own destiny, what is "coming" to us at each moment. The holds that are there, the shape of the rock, your capabilities. But this does not mean being a conformist. Not at all.

In the previous chapter we were talking about looking for opportunity. Surely, looking for opportunity will make everything more bearable, but we can also use opportunity to influence on the future: on what is happening and what will happen, and we might even be able to change it.

For this we must be certain where we can or cannot influence, what we can or cannot control. Trying to control what we cannot is an absolute waste of time and energy, as well as a constant source of frustration and other negative emotions. The Stoics knew this, which is why they strove to distinguish the things that depend on us from those that do not, in order to apply strength to the things that do depend on us, preserving peace of mind and accepting in the best possible way the things that are out of our control. This is one of the basic pillars of stoicism as a philosophy of life. It is simple to understand, but difficult to apply. We tend to overestimate the things we can control, that is, we think there are a greater number of things under our control than there really are.

> "The only things that depend on you are opinions, movements, our desires, our inclinations, our ave rsions; in a word, all our actions.
> The things that do not depend on us are body, goods, reputation, honor; in a word, everything that is not our own action."

Epictetus[21]

The only thing we can truly control is how you react to external events. If you think about it rationally, the rest is outside of your control and trying to control it or simply worrying about it is unnecessary and a waste of time and energy.

When reading the above quote people often wonder: "what does it mean my body or my reputation is not up to me? If I don't take care of them, who will?" Of course. But taking care of your body or improving it are actions, movements, inclinations. If your body gets sick or you get injured, it's independent of your choices. It is in your body. But you can take actions to prevent the loss of health or to recover it. That's where you should focus your energy, on what you can do, not on the external event that you have lost health for some reason.

Focus on the part that's up to you. If it's resting, eating right, or using your self-protection gear correctly, for example, do your best. Do everything in

---

[21] The Enchiridion, 1. Transl. Margarita Mosquera

your power, concentrating and putting aside the anxiety that would be caused by an outcome that is beyond your control.

The same with the example of reputation. You can do what you think you have to do, but you cannot control what others think of you. Because their opinions are not dependent on you, every opinion is directly dependent on the person who gives it.

Think about the fact of climbing mountains: What do you think? What does a sedentary person think? What does an older person think? Each person will have their own opinion on it, but climbing will still be a good activity for you. It doesn't matter if someone thinks it's useless or unnecessarily dangerous. You know why you do it and you shouldn't need anyone to validate it. This stoic idea helps us to turn our focus from the external things to the internal things, the things we do control, our thoughts and actions.

We come to a sector, select an interesting project and set out to try it. So how should we approach climbing from this perspective?

If the rock has few holds, it's not up to you. The grade of the route is not up to you. Even how your body feels that day is not up to you. If you are tired or have some muscle discomfort, it is part of the state of your body, which is not ultimately up to you. What depends on you is what you do from that external set of things. Your response, your actions, your attitude.

If you have an aversion to a type of climbing, let's say "overhang climbing" as an example. That aversion depends on you, it is something subjective that has nothing to do with the route itself or the grade of the route. And no matter how much you want that section you dislike to disappear, it will not. You will have to face it. And the way to deal with it will be through your actions, which are the only things that are in your control.

How do I move my attention from the things I don't control to the things I do?

By setting small realistic goals aimed at mastering what is directly under your control. Do your part and nothing else. Let's say your goal is to send a route that is slightly above your grade, has an overhanging section that you don't like at all, and you've been trying to overcome it for a long time. It is your project, your personal challenge. Achieving this objective depends to a large extent on external factors such as, for example, uncomfortable holds, complicated sequences, if there are people watching or talking around you, if the rock or temperature is not in optimal conditions, and so on. These are things that are not under your control, you can't do anything about them, so it is best not to waste time, energy and mental resources on them.

To prevent these things from affecting us, the best thing to do is to change our objectives for goals that we can achieve. They may be aligned with your ultimate goal of sending that project, but your success and satisfaction will not depend on whether you achieve it or not, because you understand that it does not depend exclusively on you.

In previous chapters we discussed that it is best to desire what we have, what comes to us (amor fati). The next step would be to desire only what is within your power, what depends on your actions. By desiring only what depends on you, you can never lose. If you want to be free of unnecessary frustrations, anxieties and fears, just focus on what you can control and forget about what you cannot.

The goal of sending the route is a way of measuring yourself against different factors that are not under your control. Identifying yourself with these external factors can only generate negative emotions. As we said earlier, the rock may be a bit wet that day, or it may be too hot, or your body may be more tired than usual because something interrupted your sleep the night before. All of this will affect your outcome, but it's not in your control. It's just the way it is. They are external things and they are not in your control. I'm not saying you shouldn't strive to send that route. Far from it. But you should focus your attention and set your goals based on what you can control. Remember that, according to the Stoics, what you can control are your desires, your opinions, your aversions and your actions.

How do I send a route by focusing only on what I can control? Your goal could be to just try the route several times in one session or to repeat the step as many times as it takes to internalize it. Train two days a week on certain moves that will help you overcome your challenge. Climb more similar routes that will make you change your attitude towards a type of rock. Develop some breathing/relaxation technique that will help you during that key step. See where I'm going? This is all in your hand. By creatively breaking down the challenge into small goals that are up to you, you will take control of your life. And, as a result, you will overcome the obstacles you set for yourself. No obstacle will stand on your way, even when factors beyond your control intervene. No matter the outcome, you have done your best every single time and you feel satisfied with yourself. Besides, you managed to send the route. That's all. It wasn't your goal. It was the consequence of your well-directed actions.

This works even in today's society. We tend to compare ourselves and compete with other people. We can even see it in climbing, when consciously or unconsciously, we measure ourselves against each other according to the grade, also with the recent relevance that competitions are gaining. You can't go around preoccupying yourself with what other people are doing. You have to concentrate on what you have to do. Create your own internal competition where you decide what matters. Learn to measure yourself with your own yardstick, assessing your capabilities based on internal goals. Work on your weaknesses as much as you need to or reinforce your strengths. Train what you feel you need to train to reach your maximum potential. When the time comes to compete, whatever was meant to happen will happen, but you will be at ease for having done your homework, having differentiated what was on your power from what was not.

Resources such as time, attention or energy are limited, we must manage them well and not waste them focusing on things that are out of our control, which are always subject to external influences. Everything external should be indifferent to you.

> "You can be invincible, if you do not engage in any combat whose victory does not depend on you."
>
> Epictetus[22]

Your persistence. Your attitude. Your actions. Concentrate on this and nothing nor anyone can defeat you. You will always get good results. You will get where you need to be and you will be satisfied that you have done your part. Start by taking responsibility for what is withing your grasp.

---

[22] The Enchiridion, 19. Transl. Margarita Mosquera

Taking responsibility

Once we learnt to accept what does not depend on us and we can discern what does, it is time to take responsibility. No more excuses, stop complaining and playing the victim. It is time to take action and be responsible for your life, for your destiny. Take the helm and steer the ship, using the winds and tides, but without drifting.

We have commented that it would be wise to ignore or be indifferent to external factors. It would be a waste of time to try to control what we cannot. The problem is that sometimes we tend to also ignore the things we can do. We ignore our responsibility, or we justify ourselves with arguments that make no sense at all when we think deeper.

Taking responsibility means doing what we can with what we have and cannot change. To do what nobody prevents you from doing, what is possible to you. Also, what nobody forces you to do. Most people tend to take responsibility only when someone or something external forces us to do so. We won't improve the way we do a task unless our boss or teacher tells us to. We won't change bad attitudes unless we argue with our partner or family member to the point of almost breaking the relationship.

Responsibility requires being critical of ourselves and our environment to identify what we can improve. And not only improving because something is wrong, but for making our life better. This way we take responsibility of your own process. Don't always depend on external circumstances that directly force you to develop and improve, but take the helm and improve yourself before external scenarios come to force you to do so.

If you know that you are not good at a certain type of climbing, you don't have to wait until you are stuck in the middle of a wall to do something about it. You can choose to take responsibility and take charge of your weaknesses before they become a problem. It's your path and you get to choose how and when you walk it. We all know that person who is always blaming everything that happens to them on others. He falls while climbing and it's the belayer's fault because they weren't giving him enough rope. Or the rock is too cold or too hot or too wet or whatever. Or others are talking and it throws him off his concentration. He will never say that his ability to concentrate failed him, it will always be something external, and therefore things he can't control. But that is not how reality works. There is always something we can do, there is always a part that is up to us and that we must analyze in order to take action. Going back to the previous example; okay, the belayer was not attentive or is not skilled enough not to interfere with your climbing. Instead of always complaining and blaming them, why not spend five minutes to teaching them specifically how you want them to belay you? How it works for you? As comfortable as it may be to always have an excuse, taking responsibility will move you forward, it will make you let go of the little barriers that keep you from doing what you want to do. Taking action, without being a passive spectator, one by one the barriers will fall. No procrastination: if you know there is something you can do, go and do it. If you know you need to climb more to improve and to develop your mental strength, go climb. Do it, even if you think it's not the perfect time or, even if it's hard. Get up and leave the comfort of your couch and go do what you have to do to become who you want to be. Now.

External things are the board, but it is you who must play the game. Figure out what your part is, what you can do within that board and make your own decisions, influence the course of events. And leave behind the laziness, fear, excuses and victimization.

We often hear statements like: I would like to do this or that, but I don't have the time. I want to exercise, but the gym is too far away. I would like to climb more, but the routes are far away or I can't train because there is no climbing gym nearby. Just as we talked about training willpower through climbing, a good willpower exercise is taking responsibility even for things you thought were unchangeable. Don't have time? Reorganize your priorities, find ways to save time by doing a task faster or eliminating distractions. Want to climb more? Look for climbing areas near you, contact your local climbing community or create one if there isn't one. Find new areas where you can practice. Set up your own climbing wall, even if it's under a bridge. Or set up a hang board at home and climb the walls of your house.

> "If you want something good, get it from yourself."
> Epictetus[23]

Don't let the current pull you around. There is always something you can do in any given situation. Sharpen your ability to differentiate what you can do and what you can't do. Tools are useless if you don't use them. And don't be shy. If you think about it, you have a much better chance than you think if you really take responsibility and are willing to pay the price, initiate the relevant actions and follow the necessary process.

> "First say to yourself what you would be; and then do what you have to do."
> Epictetus[24]

---

[23] Disertaciones por Arriano, Book I, Chapter 29. Transl Paloma Ortiz
[24] Disertaciones por Arriano, Book III, Chapter 23. Transl Paloma Ortiz

Living the process

"Nothing great is created suddenly, any more than a bunch of grapes or a fig. If you tell me that you desire a fig, I answer you that there must be time. Let it first blossom, then bear fruit, then ripen."

Epictetus[25]

In general, we tend to set a goal and then solely focus on it. We think of the process as something we need to go through and endure in order to reach our future goal. When we only pay attention to the end goal, we live in the future, despising the present moment.

But the reality is that we can only live in the present, and that the present is a continuous process. Even when we manage to reach the goals we set for ourselves, we are only halfway there. As soon as we reach the point we longed for, we are already setting our mind on the next one, thinking about other things. And there's nothing wrong with it, because life is constant change, it flows all the time and never stagnates, even if we get to where we thought we had to get to.

Therefore, if we plan on enjoying life, live in the present, let go of anxiety about the future and make the most out of every moment, we must focus on the

[25] Disertaciones por Arriano, Book I, Chapter XV. Transl Paloma Ortiz

process. We must surrender to what we can do in this instant, exploring without being attached to the results, because they may be different from what we had planned. They may even be better. When you set your goals, you couldn't know many of the things you were going to learn during the process. Your results may change as you gain new information and experience. Life is dynamic, not static. There are always factors we didn't count on and discovering them is part of the process. We need to be able to improvise, to constantly adapt. I'm not saying that you don't have to be prepared and have a goal in mind, but you have to be able to adjust to change. Surrender and trust. Let yourself be surprised by the new possibilities that open up along the way. Enjoy the journey without being attached to expectations, open to travel new paths that lead you to achieve your goal.

Our whole life is a journey, and getting somewhere is just the beginning of another journey. Driving several hours to get to the climbing area is a process. Enjoy it, discuss it with whoever accompanies you, contemplate the scenery, listen to good music. When you arrive there, it will be the beginning of another journey. Discover a new place, get relevant information, select new climbing projects. When we start climbing a route it is another journey, another process. Visualize the steps from below, try, fall, rest, learn, try again, get to the top. Fail and learn, as many times and as long as necessary. When you send the route it will be just the beginning of another project. Focus on what the present brings you, things like the new holds you can practice on that type of rock, the sensations, the environment you are in, the people you are with. Live it. Here and now. Mindfulness, I'm sure you've heard of it.

> "Concentrate every minute like a Roman — like a man— on doing what's in front of you with precise and genuine seriousness, tenderly, willingly, with justice. And on freeing yourself from all other distractions. Yes, you can— if you do everything as if it were the last thing you were doing in your life, and stop being aimless, stop letting your emotions override what your mind tells you, stop being hypocritical, self-centered, irritable. You see how few things you have to do to live a satisfying and reverent life? If you can manage this, that's all even the gods can ask of you."
>
> Marcus Aurelius[26]

Climbing is a great opportunity to learn to follow the process, to respect the order of things, the succession of small steps that lead us to the achievement of great goals. One of the best-known consequences of losing interest in the process is frustration. It is one of the most common negative emotions of our time and the one we have the hardest time dealing with. We live in immediacy, where everything is relatively easy to do or get. As soon as we want something we get it quickly.

---

[26] Meditations, Book II, 5. Transl. Gregory Hays

If I have a craving for a type of food, I can pick up the phone and have it at home in less than an hour. If I need some information, it's all there on the Internet —even if sometimes it's not entirely reliable—.

Do I feel bad? I scroll through social media or eat a picture-perfect sugary goodness and get my instant reward. This makes us used to easy and immediate rewards and we have lost interest in doing the hard things, even if they are more satisfying. We have lost interest in the process; we need the result and we need it now. But great things (with great rewards) don't happen that way. They require effort, patience and mental strength. Dealing with frustration over and over again, with being rejected, with failure, with physical limitations and with one's own limiting beliefs of what I can and cannot do. Staying firm in an intention, preserving serenity and doing one's best in every moment of the process, in every small step and even in every small setback. Resist, do not let yourself be consumed by frustration.

When someone starts climbing, the first few times they always try to take the farthest holds in order to get there faster or quicker. They hardly consider utilizing their feet to as an integral part to their progress. They don't know the process: how you can bring up a foot slightly up serves to easily reach a new hand hold that you didn't see from the previous position, to then move up the other foot and the other hand, to continue to meet the different parts of the route/

process, until you reach the top or the achievement of the goal.

"We lose the day waiting for the night, and the night fearing the dawn."

Seneca[27]

---

[27] On the shortness of life. Chapter XVI. Transl. John W. Basore

Having purpose

"If one does not know to which port one is sailing, no wind is favorable."

Seneca[28]

Following a process by persevering in our intentions can only be done when we have a clear purpose. It seems obvious, but we usually live distracted by a multitude of stimuli and fail to identify a clear purpose. Or even if we do identify our purpose, we often fail much more in identifying the path that leads us to what we want.

Having a clear purpose helps you focus on your goals, without getting distracted. Think about how what you are doing is leading you to achieve your goals and, if it doesn't, change your strategy. It's easy to do this in the middle of a route. You're climbing, following the process: one foot, one hand, another foot, another hand. It allows you to focus on the present until you achieve your goal. Also, thanks to having a clear purpose you can endure whatever it takes, because there is a reason for doing things, and if you don't choose it, someone else will choose it for you. Few people would suffer fighting against a rock,

---

[28] Letters to Lucilius. Letter LXXI. Verse 3

getting the skin of their hands peeled off and their feet crushed in tight climbing shoes if they didn't have a clear purpose.

In the simplicity of climbing we reflect on the benefits of purpose. In climbing the objective is always clear. You know that you have to climb up, that the simple and only goal is to get to the top, as high as the equipment or the mountain itself allows. You have a clear direction. The hard part is identifying and avoiding the distractions, the things that get in the way of you achieving your goal. Some distractions in climbing might be negative thoughts like "I'm not strong enough to try today," "I don't like this hold," "there's nothing to hold on to," or the unconscious fear of what others will think if I don't make it, of not meeting your own and others' expectations. There are also external things that we cannot control, such as the shape of the wall, if there are more or less people climbing with us, or if the material is optimal or not at any given moment —for example, if your climbing shoes are not the best for that moment—. All of the above are factors that influence our performance, but they are not key elements. You can be attentive to avoid recreating yourself too much in all this (this is where excuses come from) and stay focused on your purpose. Without hesitation, doing what you have to do. Align your actions with your goals. Every action will be connected to your destiny. And constantly check that you are moving the right direction.

> "The artist may have his colors all prepared, but he cannot produce a likeness unless he has already made up his mind what he wishes to paint. The reason we make mistakes is because we all consider the parts of life, but never life as a whole. The archer must know what he is seeking to hit; then he must aim and control the weapon by his skill. Our plans miscarry because they have no aim."
>
> Seneca[29]

Purpose helps you to be clear about what resources you have to mobilize to achieve something. If you know where to shoot the bow you will know how much tension to apply. If you know what port you are sailing to, you will know what wind to catch. If you know you want to climb a certain route, you will know what techniques to apply, how and when. And it will also allow you to resist what you have to resist. Be resilient, stay strong and constant towards the achievement of the goal, no matter the obstacles and difficulties. Focus your energy and resources towards a clear purpose and you will be truly efficient in whatever you set your mind to.

> "People who labor all their lives but have no purpose to direct every thought and impulse toward are wasting their time —even when hard at work."
>
> Marcus Aurelius[30]

---

[29] Moral Letters to Lucilius. Letter LXXI. Verse 2. Transl. Richard M. Gummere
[30] Meditations, Book II, 7. Transl. Gregory Hays

Memento Mori

Remember that you will die. And not to make you sad, but quite the opposite. Be glad to be alive. Imagine that you know you will die soon and that there is nothing you can do, wouldn't you live today to the fullest? Wouldn't you take advantage of every little occasion to do whatever it is that satisfies you or surround yourself with people you feel good with? Almost certainly. Well, the reality is that, although we may not be aware of it because we don't think about it, we are going to die. Maybe not soon, but we will. Every day we are a little closer to death, and there is no going back.

The Stoics often meditated on death. They thought it served to clarify their ideas and motivations, to make the best use of of the present moment, to find joy more easily and to be grateful for the simple fact of being alive. They reflected about change and the transience of life.

Everything is in continuous movement and nothing should be taken for granted. What was yesterday may not be today. This is neither good nor bad, it is simply important to remember to enjoy what every moment grants us and not to think of moments as infinite, because, if there is something really clear in this world, it is that everything changes.

"Observe always that everything is the result of a change, and get used to thinking that there is nothing Nature loves so well as to change existing forms and to make new ones like them."

Marcus Aurelius[31]

Remember that everything you do, every moment you live, could be your last. And not necessarily because you die, but because nothing like it will ever happen again. If you live it fully you will feel good with the memory of it, you will let it go when it is time knowing that you have done everything you had to do.

You don't have to live in fear of what might happen, you simply have to live the moment, don't risk it passing over and missing the party. Death and change are totally natural and everyday processes. We should not be afraid of them and pretend they do not exist, we must be aware and do the best we can in each moment, knowing the rules of the game.

"When we cease from activity, or follow a thought to its conclusion, it's a kind of death. And it doesn't harm us. Think about your life: childhood, boyhood, youth, old age. Every transformation a kind of dying. Was that so terrible?"

Marcus Aurelius[32]

Life is a journey that only goes one direction. Do

[31] Meditations, Book IV, 36
[32] Meditations, Book IX, 21. Transl. Gregory Hays

what you have to do in each moment, enjoy and experience each thing, without putting it off until tomorrow or thinking it will be infinite. Because we tend to do that, we tend to think that things don't change and that they last forever. And the truth is that they always change, and if they don't change, it is us who change. We tend to procrastinate, to think that everything we could have done today we can also do tomorrow. Then, our lazy, comfort-loving mind often prefers to stay on the couch under the pretext that we are tired or don't have time, instead of getting out there and living the life that is happening (and passing away, changing) at this very moment and not in another. If your friends are suggesting a plan or an interesting trip, go with them! They may each have their own life tomorrow (start a family, for example) and never suggest something to do together again. If a partner wants to go climbing, then go! Maybe tomorrow their schedule will not coincide with yours or they will have to change cities. If you want to visit a certain place, stop saying so and go! It may not be there tomorrow; it may be overcrowded or it may have lost its charm for whatever reason. If you want to climb a route, go and do it! Enjoy it now, tomorrow you may be different and not have the ability you have today to enjoy it; you may have evolved and be at a higher level and, therefore, you are enjoying other things, or you have an injury or come from a period of inactivity and you are not able to do it.

Think about your past, all the things you would have liked to do but you didn't. What were you thinking? You probably thought you could do it later. And you were wrong.

Would you have made more of an effort to enjoy the now whenever you reflected on the possibility that something might be different in the future? Probably. And it applies to everything. Everything is subject to change, to death, to movement. And it can happen gradually, or be unexpected.

> "Let us prepare our minds as if we'd come to the very end of life. Let us postpone nothing. Let us balance life's books each day. ... The one who puts the finishing touches on their life each day is never short of time."
>
> Seneca[33]

Remember when you were in lockdown how much you missed going out to the mountains? Would you have enjoyed your last outing more if you knew you wouldn't be able to go for so long?

You might get injured or sick and it might keep you from doing what you love. Being aware that our situation can change at any moment helps us to stop procrastinating on life. To stop making excuses (such as "I don't have time", which in the end is just laziness in disguise) and to do what you have to do every day, without leaving unfinished business.

---

[33] Letters to Lucilius, Letter CI. Verse 7

Imagine the feeling of going out climbing with your favorite people after a week of intense work or just bad weather. Sharing a sunset, taking a walk in nature —how simple and how hard it is for us to incorporate it into our busy lives!

Become aware of the change and let this help you to enjoy everything you do in each precise moment. Everything flows, everything passes. Even what we judge as "bad" —even though, with our amor fati, we know how to turn our judgments around—.

> "Frightened of change? But what can exist without it? What's closer to nature's heart? Can you take a hot bath and leave the firewood as it was? Eat food without transforming it? Can any vital process take place without something being changed? Can't you see? It's just the same with you —and just as vital to nature."
>
> Marcus Aurelius[34]

In fact, the Stoics had a technique for this, to help them become aware that something can change or go wrong from one moment to the next, so they had to appreciate what they had at this very moment and, moreover, be prepared to lose it.

Unlike today's motivational currents that urge us to visualize positive outcomes, probably in order to have a clear purpose, the Stoics did the opposite: they visualized negative possibilities. And it's not that they wanted bad things to happen. They preferred to be aware that any situation could turn bad, end

---

[34] Meditations, Book VII, 18. Transl. Gregory Hays

or change. This made them appreciate the present moment as much as they could, and, in turn, be prepared in case bad things do happen.

In climbing we are familiar with visualization. It is a useful tool to simulate the steps we are going to take on a route, internalize movements and gain confidence. We look at the wall and our brain projects an image of us climbing it, with greater or lesser details. We normally visualize ourselves executing the steps correctly and having a successful climb. But sometimes our mind plays tricks on us and reflects possibilities that we do not really want. If there is a step or a sequence that we believe to be difficult, our mind prepares us for the fall by projecting that image in reality. We will have a predisposition to fall just by believing (or visualizing) that we are going to fall. Our body will be more prepared to receive a fall than to reach for the hold we needed. But this is not the type of visualization we are talking about in this chapter.

The premeditatio malorum of the Stoics was more of a reflection, a pause to think about all the possibilities in order to appreciate more what there is and yet prepare to lose it (or have it change).
Imagining how something could be worse helps us appreciate it more for what it is. Don't let your head wander to what is not, how you would like it to be or ruminate on unnecessary desires. Instead find and enjoy things as they are. If you are climbing a new

route and you find an uncomfortable hold, imagine if it were even smaller, or if the foot holds were worse, or if an eventual fall was poorly protected. How much would this change your perception, your attitude towards "what is"? I bet you would be more grateful for what seemed bad to you before, simply by imagining something worse.

> "You could leave life right now. Let that determine what you do and say and think."
>
> Marcus Aurelius[35]

Certainly, one should not live constantly thinking about negative possibilities. It would be impossible to drive thinking that we are going to have an accident. It would be impossible to climb if we constantly think about how hard it might be or that we might fall. But it doesn't hurt reflecting on them from time to time. We need to contemplate these things more often. It grounds you before something knocks you off your feet. And it will make you more grateful for what is already there, compared to the possibility that it might not be there or might be different. How many times have you reflected on the existence of the mountains, the people around you or the things you like? We usually believe that they are there because they have to be there, because we deserve them or because they are the way we conceive them to be. But the reality is that it could be different, indeed,

---

[35] Meditations, Book II. 11. Transl. Gregory Hays

they can change at any moment.

Nothing and no one is immune to change, transformation. Sometimes we think that our life is totally stable, that nothing ever happens, and so we walk around overly confident and without paying too much attention to our surroundings. This is also what makes negative visualization useful: to be prepared and attentive. In climbing it is always useful to have a dose of visualizing negative possibilities from time to time. Overconfidence is the main cause of climbing accidents. Perhaps thinking more often about what could happen would also help us to prevent it, to avoid accidents. Do what is in our power —what depends on me— to prevent misfortunes. Use the material better, communicate better with others or analyze our possibilities more objectively. This technique would not only make us appreciate life more, but will make us be more aware of the risks we face, and get us to think about how we should act if any of the negative things we reflected on were to happen.

This allows you to empower yourself. By imagining that something you fear happens, you can see that it's not as bad as you thought. That there would be something you could do about it. That you could adapt to the new situation. It is freeing to know you are capable because you have reflected on your abilities and you know they are there for you. It eliminates unnecessary worries and makes you lighter, freer to enjoy the experience knowing the risks. You become more confident in what you do because you know the real cost, without being driven by the most irrational fears. In climbing, when you are afraid of falling and this fear prevents you from moving forward, from risking to try a move and leaves you paralyzed on the wall. And when you think about it calmly, a fall would not even be that serious. You could withstand it perfectly well, taking the necessary measures to protect yourself. But fear is there, limiting your experience, making you miss out on life because you fear something. You miss out on the experience of progressing, of overcoming your limits and achieving your goals; and that is much worse than a simple, well-protected fall.

> "It is not death that a man should fear, but he should fear never beginning to live."
>
> Marcus Aurelius[36]

---

[36] Meditations, Book XII, 1.

The social aspect

Although it may give the impression that climbing is a solitary activity —the climber and the mountain— the reality is quite different. We often see spectacular images of an epic climber holding on to impossible holds and performing precise moves at high altitude, but they don't show us everything that's behind it. All the people behind it. As in almost every activity we can think of, sharing with other people is an intrinsic part of climbing: our partners with whom we go out on the rock, with whom we train, those who belay us with the responsibility of having our life in their hands, the rest of the climbers we meet by chance, our close environment (even if they don't share our interests), route setters, the people who bolt the routes or those who inspire us through texts, photographs and impressive videos.

The climbing tribe is definitely one of the most interesting ones you could belong to. People who internalize the values of climbing and love to live and share them. Anyone who has interacted with people in front of the walls will know what I'm talking about. They may be unbearable people in their day to day lives (I doubt it, but they can be). Climbing seems to have the ability to align people around values. Or, for some reason, to attract a particular type of person. If only our daily interactions with other people were as satisfying as the ones we have on the mountain. Still, it has its tense moments like any other social activity. Let's look at some stoic techniques for dealing with the rest of the world in any circumstance, and in this case, climbing.

As we have seen in previous chapters, everything has two handles on which to hold on. One is bearable, and the other is difficult and uncomfortable. Following the maxim of making the best of every situation (as we discussed in the chapter on opportunity) it is best to focus on the good side of those interactions, as well as accepting and learning to deal with the negative side of them.

The good side is the positive experiences we have with others around climbing. The people who belay, motivate or inspire us. The people who design new routes for everyone to enjoy or share information with others. Marcus Aurelius had an interesting technique for taking his relationships on the good side and appreciating them as much as possible. He used to reflect on the different positive qualities of the people around him in order to be inspired and in turn be grateful for what those people bring to him. He would begin his personal journal —which after his death became the Meditations— with as many as seventeen sections reflecting and giving thanks in this way:

"1- From my grandfather Verus, good morals and the government of my temper.

2 - From the reputation and remembrance of my father, modesty and a manly character.

3 - From my mother, piety and beneficence, and abstinence, not only from evil deeds, but even from evil thoughts; and further, simplicity in my way of living, far removed from the habits of the rich…"

Marcus Aurelius[37]

You can also be inspired by the people around you or even by people you admire without knowing them personally. When climbing, you can be inspired by the ability of an unknown climber to try again and again without getting discouraged, by the attitude of a fellow climber in the face of difficulties, by the way someone else deals with frustration, or by the ability of the person belaying you to keep calm. In this way, besides appreciating more the people around you and the activity you are doing, you will be able to internalize a series of desirable qualities for yourself. That is to say, only by observing the qualities of others do you open up the possibility of developing them, since in this way you know them, you know if they work or not, or if it would be good for you to work on them. You expose yourself to them deliberately and they influence you. You learn to appreciate certain ways of being or doing and, as a result, you can set yourself the goal of developing your capabilities.

It is not about comparing ourselves with others, it

---

[37] Meditations, Book I. 1.1/1.2/1.3. Transl. Pierre Hadot

is about reflecting on what works for others and inspires them. Learn to identify it to be aware that it is possible, that it is something we can develop ourselves. In any person you can find a good quality to reflect on, something they do better than you and that you can admire and work towards.

But as you know, in social relationships it's not all that smooth. Tensions arise more often than we would like. Different people, different expectations, different ways of seeing the world. In life we will encounter all kinds of people and situations that we cannot control and that do not depend on our actions, but they can still help us to exercise our mental strength, so that we always maintain the much-appreciated serenity. As already pointed out in previous chapters, the rest of the people, their actions, thoughts and opinions, are not within the group of things that depend on us, so, according to the Stoics, the best thing would be to ignore them completely and focus on what we can control, such as, for example, our opinions towards others, towards what they do or think.

We live in times when everyone has an opinion about everything and everyone. With the internet and the amount of information available, almost everyone believes they are in a position to judge the lives or actions of others. And, as a bonus, we also live in a time when everyone is offended by everything, a kind of social hypersensitivity or low tolerance for criticism and different opinions. What a recipe for unhappiness: a lot of people giving their opinions about others who get offended, and, at the same time, a lot of offended people giving their opinions about other people. And so on to infinity in a spiral of chronic dissatisfaction.

To break this dynamic, the Stoics proposed some ways to deal with criticism or insults, always acting from what depends on yourself. If you receive a criticism or insult, before taking it badly, think about whether there is any truth in it. If there is some truth in the insult or criticism, you can take it as feedback, as valuable information that you receive and that helps you to improve. Imagine, for example, that someone is picking on you because you are taking a hold that belongs to another route, showing that you are climbing the route in a way that is perhaps easier or even more risky in the face of a possible fall. If you weren't aware of this, you'll appreciate it being pointed out to you. If you were aware and want to do it that way for some reason, you should not be offended if someone pointed it out to you. There is no need to be offended because someone expresses an opinion or highlights something you are doing wrong. And if you disagree that something you are doing is wrong, you can simply explain it patiently until your point is understood. Or, even simpler, accept that there are different opinions and ignore it. It also depends on who is doing the criticizing. If it is the partner with whom you spend most of your time, it might be more convenient to dialogue and work to be on the same page and to have similar points of view, since you will be sharing different situations. It is more interesting to learn together than to be right or wrong.

Analyzing the source of the criticism serves to see if it is worth dialoguing or simply ignoring, as well as to see if the person issuing the criticism is an authority for you. If the criticism comes from a respectable source, you are more likely to accept the criticism and value the information. You are more likely to take it as an opportunity to improve. However, if on reflection you realize that the person making the criticism is not a good source of information, it is better to simply ignore it or take it with humor. If you're climbing and a casual hiker comes along and tells you that you're crazy for hanging off the wall, I don't think it's a criticism you should take too seriously. On the other hand, if an experienced climber comes along and tells you that you're crazy because you're using the gear incorrectly, you'd better take the criticism and do something about it. Even be grateful.

> "If someone succeeds in provoking you, realize that your mind is complicit in the provocation."
>
> Epictetus[38]

Remember that you do not need external approval.

---
[38] The Enchiridion, 20

You have to focus on what depends on yourself, set your own realistic goals in accordance with your capabilities, without depending on what others think. Do what you want to do without being conditioned by external opinion, which is also changeable and, on many occasions, not entirely well-intentioned.

It seems simple and we may even think that we apply it, but if we take a moment to analyze it, the truth is that it is not always so. On more occasions than we would like to admit, we are conditioned by external validation. By the search for social status, by what others may think of us or by the fear of the image we may project.

With the rise of social media, this trend towards seeking external recognition and status is becoming even more pronounced. We all know climbers who every time they go out to the rock you can tell that they care too much about taking pictures of themselves. Do they climb because they really like it or what they really like are the likes and social recognition?

> "Who are those people by whom you wish to be admired? Are they not these whom you are in the habit of saying that they are mad? What then? Do you wish to be admired by the mad?"
>
> Epictetus[39]

Social recognition can be something that motivates us, something that validates us and makes us feel good

---

[39] Disertaciones por Arriano, Book I. Chapter XX. Transl. Paloma Ortiz

about ourselves and our environment, but at the same time, it is a source of anxiety and frustration. Always trying to fit into the image that others have of you is a sure failure because it is something external and each person has their standards, their opinions, their criteria. Trying to fit in with everyone would be a good way to develop insanity.

There are climbers who are obsessed with the grade, with sending more routes, and, in addition, judge the value of others with their own standards. Or they are afraid to repeat a route they have already sent, in case they fail this time and someone thinks they are losing their qualities. If you want to keep your peace of mind, you should not let yourself be measured by the standards of others. A person may be better at one type of rock or another, or in on-sight climbing, using more strength or more balance and flexibility. Or simply enjoy what they do to the fullest, much more than those who allow themselves to be measured by others and try to please other people's expectations.

You have to live according to yourself and no one else. You can be inspired by others and share your life with others, but don't let yourself be influenced too much by what others think, or try to do things because other people approve of them. Or not try them for fear of what others will say. Everyone knows their own truth and why they do what they do. Anyone who has never climbed before will think it's pointlessly dangerous. But you know why you do it and the benefits it brings you, so you don't really need someone who thinks that to validate you to continue enjoying your practice.

The Stoics thought that no one intended to do evil to other people. They did not think that others were evil, they simply considered them ignorant, that they did not know any other way. Lacking in wisdom. That each person, within their own internal motivations, had a good reason for doing what they do. The problem is that, generally, people lack the wisdom necessary to make that reason for doing things beneficial to the greatest possible number of people. If you observe that someone is abusing or misusing the equipment on a wall, at the belay station, for example, that person probably doesn't know any other way to use it. Maybe they are not skilled enough to use it better, or they don't know that they should use their own material (or how to use it) instead of the communal material that is on the rock, which belongs to everyone, and it is our responsibility to use it well. The wear and tear of the material is something that affects everyone who enjoys a specific route, and when someone doesn't use their own material to protect that of the community is incumbent on everyone, including the subject in question. But most likely that person is not doing so with intent to abuse the material. More likely, they don't know that it should be done differently, or simply don't know how to do it.

Then, starting from the things that depend on ourselves, we can arm ourselves with patience and explain it in the best possible way to change the situation, and thus benefit all of us: both the person who you take out of their ignorance and help them to develop their practical knowledge, and the rest of the climbing community that will enjoy a material in good condition for longer.

Another example might be someone who is continually criticizing and commenting on the actions of others. It may give the impression that they are doing this in bad faith, but it is probably their way of trying to help or reflect on their surroundings and external events. It is their ignorance about the expectations of others that may make that person irritable, but not their bad intentions.

All this simply refers to the concept of amor fati as applied to social relationships. The idea that people cannot be any other way than the way they are, and it is useless to expect something different. You cannot be surprised that a fig tree bears figs, as Marcus Aurelius would say. What would be strange is if it produced pears. So it is with people. You will always find people who will be impertinent, who will criticize you without grounds or without knowing you, or who will try to influence your life with their opinions. That's just the way it is. Generally, people tend to be negative. Fortunately, you have the mental strength and resources —such as those outlined in this book— to deal with these types of individuals. Besides, it is up to you to know how to differentiate good company from bad company, avoiding complainers and excessive negativity for the sake of your serenity.

> "Begin each day by telling yourself: today I shall be meeting with interference, ingratitude, insolence, disloyalty, ill-will, and selfishness—all of them due to the offenders' ignorance of what is good or evil. But for my part I have long perceived the nature of good and its nobility, the nature of evil and its meanness, and also the nature of the culprit himself, who is my brother (not in the physical sense, but as a fellow-creature similarly endowed with reason and a share of the divine); therefore none of those things can injure me, for nobody can implicate me in what is degrading. Neither can I be angry with my brother or fall foul of him; for he and I were born to work together, like a man's two hands, feet, or eyelids, or like the upper and lower rows of his teeth. To obstruct each other is against Nature's law—and what is irrational or aversion but a form of obstruction?"
>
> Marcus Aurelius[40]

We are a social species; we are made for collaboration. In fact, it is precisely the ability to collaborate that has brought us to where we are today. It is what differentiates us from our cousins the apes. Climbing wouldn't exist if we didn't trust each other, if we weren't able to work together to break new routes or find new ways of doing things, if we didn't rely

[40] Meditations, Book II, 1. Transl. Ramón Bach

on information provided by others or routes already opened.

The fact that someone opens a new climbing area or a new sector is good for the whole community, since more people will be able to enjoy climbing and the richer and more varied the environment will be. At the same time, the more likely it is that someone who starts in the new sector will open a new one later on, collaborate in its maintenance or that of a climbing gym, or bring new perspectives to it. But beware, it also works the other way around. If you do something wrong or harmful to others, you are also harming yourself. If, for example, you do not respect your environment, dirtying or destroying the ecosystem of the other living beings that live in the climbing sectors, you will cause a negative reaction to the activity itself, over-regulating and prohibiting the opening of new sectors or closing access to those that already exist. We are all on the same team.

"What does not benefit the hive, is no benefit to the bee."
Marcus Aurelio[41]

---

[41] Meditations, Book VI, 54. Transl. A. S. L. Farquharson

Everything is connected

"Keep reminding yourself of the way things are connected, of their relatedness. All things are implicated in one another and in sympathy with each other. This event is the consequence of some other one. Things push and pull on each other, and breathe together, and are One."

Marcus Aurelius[42]

Forget what you think you are. The stories your ego tells you about yourself and the world. Be humble in front of a big piece of rock. Challenge yourself and remember how small you are compared to the world, but, at the same time you are big because you can navigate in it as part of it. You can climb the rock, using your body and the techniques developed over the years by you and others. Climb while being perfectly aware of the vastness of the world, looking down from above while you are a tiny speck in the middle of a big wall.

When you are at the top of a mountain, after a successful climb, take your time and realize how every little step, every effort and every experience has brought you to where you are at that very moment. You will feel deeply grateful for the present moment and for all that makes it possible.

[42] Meditations, Book VI, 38. Transl. Gregory Hays

You can feel the connection to all of humanity and how you are the result of it. Think about how people work and spend their time and money establishing new routes for total strangers to enjoy as well. Think about how your partner inspires you with enough confidence to tie your rope, and your life, to them. Or how they encourage you when you have any weak thoughts. That special connection you have with people on the mountain, in the natural environment that brings out the best in humans and maximizes the experience of interconnectedness.

At your body's micro level, you can reflect on the same concept by paying attention to how you need to use your body as a whole to climb well and fluidly. That is, coordinating not only your hands with your feet, but the position of your hips, whether you should throw more of your body weight to the opposite side of the hold in order to use it or sway from side to side like the course of a river, which goes from one meander to another bouncing and zigzagging in a sinuous way, meandering and seeking its balance all the way to the sea. Be aware of your own "universe within your body", your microcosm, how in climbing you must harmonize your whole body and mind to flow with the rock.

Everything has influence on everything else, that's why you have to be responsible for your actions. You wouldn't harm your left hand to benefit your right hand just as you don't harm others and the rest of the environment because you know they are part of you. One hand holds the weight of your body so that the other can move, so alternately one grips and one expands, complementing each other like all things in the universe, even though for some reason we humans tend to believe we are superior or outside of natural laws. If only until the next pandemic.

With climbing, it is easy to feel what they call "oceanic feeling": a sense of eternity, a feeling of being one with the world. Of infinity. Of how everything is connected and part of the whole. How every element, no matter how small, has a function and an impact. Feel it. Feel the wind, the rock, your hands, the cold or the heat, the views over the horizon, the birds flying.... Get out of your little tunnel of reality where you only see your routines, your problems, your difficulties or your pleasures and reconnect with the immensity, with the cosmic perspective that we are an insignificant dot in the universe and yet we are important as we are part of it and its system. The universe as a whole is all part of a unique and indivisible organism in constant flux, a kind of infinite ecosystem that is constantly changing and yet always maintaining a particular balance.

Everything is connected, you with others, the present with the future, the sun with the plants, the plants with each other through a mycelial network, the sea with the clouds, nature with humans, and so on. Because of that connection you can find beauty everywhere, in every little thing, from the most impressive rock wall to the smallest flower, the lizard sunbathing next to you, or the tree sinking its roots into the rock drinking the seeping water and giving new forms to the mountain.

Just stop. Get out of your head and look around you, recognize the beauty of all things and be grateful for the possibility to enjoy it. Feel the joy of being alive and belonging to the world, of being part of something great.

Throughout this book we have seen how the thoughts of people who lived, suffered and enjoyed more than two thousand three hundred years ago can be applied to today, to the practice of climbing. The connection between past and present, ancient and modern, climbing and life. To the experience of climbing and your life in general, every area, every situation, every experience is part of a whole, and by simply trying to improve the conscious experience, even if only in one part (climbing), that development will spill over into all areas of your life. Wake up to the world and the immense possibilities for growth it offers. And take action. For example, through climbing.

It's all in the mind

In climbing, as in life, we tend to overlook the power of the mind. It's not that we can levitate and climb walls just by thinking about it, but neither are we a powerless nutshell in the ocean, at the mercy of the waves, with no control.

Everything, absolutely everything, has to pass through the filter of your mind. This is why the mind is much more powerful than you think. And when you have such a powerful weapon or tool, it is better to dedicate some intention to learn how to use it and control it, so it doesn't end up harming us more than benefiting us. We wouldn't want to be constantly shooting ourselves with our own weapon.

I bet you are saying: "yes, yes, the power of the mind is very strong, but if I don't have the physical strength to hold on to a grip or to progress vertically, I'm not going to do much with my mind". Correct. But in your mind is the strength to train harder and better, to resist frustration, to pursue a goal, keep trying and achieve what you set out to do. In the mind is to stay calm and explore the rock until you find the right sequence. In the mind you can find the necessary tools. You just have to pay the price of learning to master a wild mind that avoids discomfort, that is used to sabotage your purposes with all kinds of self-deceptions and perverse techniques such as insisting on the difficulty of things, focusing on the negative side or on what you cannot control and undermining your determination towards a set goal.

A mind that has not been "tamed" is like a wild elephant in a shopping mall. Wherever it goes it will destroy everything, whether it is a clothing store or a restaurant. However, a well-worked, well-tamed mind has the same strength as the elephant, only it can use it as it pleases for whatever it wants. And no, you don't have to take it to the mall if that's not its place. You can respect it and take it to its natural habitat, to its main purpose, that is: reason. Because the mind was made to think, to reason, to be used, to work and to reflect, even if sometimes it is lazy and seeks the easy way without caring about the suffering it generates. Remember, an untamed mind will always prefer to sleep a couple of hours more than getting up early to climb walls, even if the latter brings you more benefits —in terms of health, satisfaction or mental strength, for example— and you know it.

The Stoics called it living in agreement with nature. And they were not referring to walking around naked and climbing trees (as awesome as this might be) but to the ability to reason inherent in human nature and which has brought us so many advantages throughout history —as well as so many tensions and suffering for ignoring it or not knowing/wanting to master it—. The stoic concept of "nature" is very complex and also alludes to the universal order of things and how they are constantly changing and flowing, but it also has a lot to do with how we use our mental strength and serenity to deal with our environment in the best possible way.

We have the innate potential to do what is best for ourselves and others, to change, grow and develop, along with the ability to reason to find ways to do so. Whether we do or not is up to us. We decide how we filter reality through our mind and what we do from those perceptions. We decide on reflecting and doing what we have to do without regrets: face on and with determination.

The ancient Greeks called it *Areté*, which could be translated as "excellence" and consists of working, always and at all times, to be the best version of ourselves. It implies that every decision and action we take is aimed at manifesting what we believe to be the ideal self. Align what you want with what you say and what you do. Use your strength of character (mental strength) to straighten your life towards your best goals, towards what you want to be, towards your happiness, without letting yourself be carried away by the things that we know that take us away from the path.

"A good character is the only guarantee of everlasting, care-free happiness. Even if some obstacle to this comes on the scene, its appearance is only to be compared to that of clouds which drift in front of the sun without ever defeating its light."

Seneca[43]

---

[43] Letters from a Stoic, Letter XXVII. Transl. Robin Campbell

Practical summary

You get out of bed not without effort, abandoning comfort, but knowing that adventure, life, awaits you. You could sleep in for a couple more hours or stay at home watching TV shows, but you choose to live. You know that life is more than comfort, security and entertainment, even if sometimes it's hard to remember. You know it's worth the effort. In fact, you're passionate about doing it. You have expanded your comfort zone so much that you come to the mountain and you feel at home, you appreciate everything it has to offer and you don't mind the "inconveniences". You appreciate the fresh air, the birds flying, the views, the tranquility or the physical challenge it poses. And you are absolutely indifferent to the discomfort, having to eat sitting on a rock, getting dirty, not having electricity, running water or reception on your phone.

You arrive at the crag, you look at the routes. At first, as you are a bit lazy because you still have the mark of the sheets on your face, you get the impression that they are quite difficult, that it's going to be a tough day. You want to select your next project or projects, but until you get your hands on the rock and warm up a bit, your perception is a bit clouded with limitations.

So, you warm up on an easy route and gradually you wake up, gaining objectivity about what you can actually do or not do. Now you are able to look directly at things and evaluate reality more objectively. Observe the rock, the types of holds, the possible sequences, your physical condition. Your mind begins to clear, to gain clarity.

It's time to choose your next challenge. You evaluate your possibilities, you visualize it from below. You accept all the sequences you can find, without considering whether they are easy or difficult. You only think about how you think they should be done, making the effort to reflect, avoiding that past impressions or experiences condition your judgment. In each route there will be sequences that we will like more or less, more complicated or less, or that involve more psychological tension for whatever reason. But that is precisely the beauty of the route, its variety and diversity, its flow and acceptance of what is coming until the experience is complete. It is what it is, the wall is what it is and that is the price you have to pay to overcome the challenge, to push your limits a little further. Live it as it is.

And the time comes, you get your hands on the rock, you start climbing. You make progress, easily clipping all the bolts, following the process towards your clear goal, to reach the meeting without falling or resting, to send the route you have set for yourself, using your physical and mental strength, your ability to interpret the impressions you get from the rock and act accordingly, to use the necessary techniques to progress effectively. You climb one foot here, one hand there, you clip, you move a foot, you look for a hand, it gets more and more complicated, you have to spend more time looking for the sequence. Your energy starts to dwindle, there are only a few meters to go, you are approaching the key step. And you fall. You fail. But it doesn't cause you any frustration. You know it's part of the process and you accept it. You reflect and come up with a new hypothesis of how the step should be tackled and you try it again. You fall again. "What could be going wrong? Am I placing my foot, hands or body wrong? Am I lacking the strength and/or technique to perform that type of grip? Am I unfocused?"

You realize that the goal of sending the route depends on too many factors, and some of them you can't control or even don't know, so you change your goal to something that is in your hand, something you can do right now: seize the opportunity to improve. Look for weaknesses, for your most obvious limitations and analyze and address them, tackle them. Thanks to your failure and the challenge of the route, you can improve yourself, you can practice and improve new grips, look for new footholds or new ways of doing the same sequence.

Discover and further develop your potential. Amor Fati. It was what it had to be. Thanks to this moment and this opportunity you will be able to climb more and better in the future, enjoying a satisfying present.

You try again. From the bottom. Focusing only on what depends on you, i.e. how you manage your energy, resting in the most comfortable holds along the route, without wasting in easy movements. Efficiently. But you fail again, you fall. This time even before the key step. A wave of negative emotions like anger or frustration is about to wash over you. Your mind is spinning out of control and you start looking for excuses to justify why expectations are not being met. You look to blame something external, your belayer you thought was distracted, the rock, or a fly that landed on your face. But you catch it quickly and break the loop. You take responsibility for yourself, for your present and the possibilities, without devoting more thought to what is external to you and even less to making excuses to justify yourself to yourself and others. It is not necessary. It is not useful. Do what you have to do. Reflect and try harder and better. That's where you have to focus your attention. You don't care about the result, you just want to enjoy the process, try, experiment, learn. Enjoying every step in every moment, little by little you will be closer to the top. You will be in a position to overcome the barriers, to unite all the sections, cornering your weaknesses and putting them to work, turning them into strength. And, in the end, you make it. It was inevitable. Action after action, there was no other possibility.

You take a breath, you rest there hanging, you celebrate your achievement. You feel grateful for everything that has made you get where you are, for your companions, for nature, for your mind, your body, for the whole community of climbers who make the activity bigger and bigger. What a joy to be alive! To be able to climb, to observe nature, to merge with it, to put our body and mind to work, that's what we have them for anyways.

You think you're even going to miss the route, the challenge it posed, working on it. Although you can always repeat it again, it is already part of the past, and it's okay, you can let it go because you have enjoyed it and worked on it as you should, without reservations and without anything left to do. You are ready to change, to start again on another route and enjoy another process, another challenge.

Portrait of the stoic climber

At first glance the stoic climber is no different from anyone else. They're probably not the strongest, the one who goes to the rock the most, or the one who does the highest grade. They're just another person enjoying the activity. The difference is on the inside, in their head. In their way of doing and not doing. It doesn't matter what level they're working at; it doesn't matter if they're trying their first leading route or if they're comfortable in the hardest routes. What makes the difference is how they take things, how they manage themselves and their possibilities.

They are able to analyze the situation clearly and precisely and then mobilize the necessary resources and tools. They are also an optimist. They have a good attitude towards what they perceive. They know that by applying the necessary reflection and effort they have a good chance of achieving what they set out to do. But, despite their optimism, they are at the same time aware of the negative possibilities, so they do everything in their power to climb as safely as possible, to be prepared and to prevent any unforeseen event as far as possible. They stay grounded in reality and do not get carried away by overconfidence. It certainly takes a good dose of stoicism to pull your hand out of a precarious grip to try to catch something higher up, not knowing if it will be a good hold or not, or even if you will hit it correctly to be able to hold on to the wall.

When they have to face a new challenge, a new project, they see the opportunity to put into practice everything they know about life and the search for serenity. They are always alert to their perceptions, they observe them closely to prevent their mind from sabotaging their intentions or manipulating their experience.

They concentrate to align their mind and body with their new goal. In turn, they unpack it as if they were different pieces of a puzzle. And they see clearly which of those pieces are directly dependent on them. Energy management, attempts they make, information they gather, training they need, and so on. They also know which ones do not depend on them, so as not to waste their energy and resources in vain.

If there is something that makes them especially uncomfortable, they go for it. They expose themselves. They expand their comfort zone. Because that's life. Easy living brings more trouble and dissatisfaction than pleasure or happiness. The last thing they would want is to be a frustrated person for not having made the effort to develop their potential. That's why they enjoy solving difficult things.

Overcoming challenges, climbing walls. Taking the opportunity to improve on every obstacle or difficulty they encounter along the way.

That's why they work hard for what they want. But they are not a donkey that pushes forward no matter what. They reflect, they think. They change their strategy if necessary, but they persist. They don't stick to expectations, to results or to repeating wrong patterns. Instead, they take responsibility for their failures and their possibilities and try new things, experiment, explore new paths. With the humility of the one who knows that they do not know everything. That they are in a constant process of learning and discovering, of exploring.

Precisely because of this, because they know they are part of a process, they have a high tolerance for frustration. They know that there may be something they are not doing well at the moment, or that they are finding it harder than they expected. But that's the game, and you have to play it to learn (and to win). They don't despair if they still can't do something or something isn't going the way they'd like it to. If a move doesn't go well, or if their fear is conditioning them too much, they don't get discouraged, they simply have patience and do what they have to do so that at some point things will move towards their goal.

They fully enjoy the moment, the part of the process they are in, because they know it will pass.

And it won't come back. Whatever that moment is. Whether they are working hard to figure out the next move or they just untied themselves after achieving their goal. They know how to appreciate each moment as part of a whole that makes them move forward, grow and gain mental strength and serenity at the same time. They realized that they can only live within themselves, so in the end they have become accustomed to and like the things that happen to them, they learn from everything, from everyone and from themselves, constantly.

With respect to the external, such as social relations, they apply more or less the same principles as to their climbing. They know how to differentiate between what depends on them and what does not. Criticism does not offend them. They know that the judgments that another person may have based on their perceptions are not in their hands, although they don't mind reflecting on the feedback received if they consider that it may be useful to them or that it comes from someone they really respect. At the base of it all is not looking for external validation. Having your own internal motivation to do what you do and not depending on whether others approve it. Let's say they can spend the day climbing without taking a single photo. It's not that they don't want to share their experience with others, it's that they have their own measure to interpret the beauty of the situation, regardless of the potential likes.

For those who know how to look and are aware of the connection of all things, everything has some kind of beauty. It is the result of some natural process, perfect in itself and in its own way. From the great mountains and valleys that we can observe from the top of the walls to the smallest rock formations, with their cracks caused by millions of years of erosion and subjection to natural forces. Or the plants that mix their aroma with the air or the breeze that refreshes your efforts on the wall. For the rest of the people whose effort and motivation made it possible for you to enjoy all that.

For everything, the stoic climber is mainly a person grateful to life, able to appreciate even the smallest nuances and enjoy them, without taking them for granted at any time. And they know that not everything is easy and comfortable, they are also aware of the difficulties, to which they respond by fighting, persisting and growing in adversity and obstacle without losing the same humble attitude and ability to maintain serenity to do what they have to do, what they believe is right and courageous. Wisdom as a vital motivation.

Nor do they mind sharing their wisdom, their discoveries and their reflections with others to promote the growth of the rest of the people who are part of the global village or even to further stimulate their reflection through healthy debate, although they will always be careful enough not to inflate their ego by boasting of their stoicism or believing themselves superior to the rest who may have difficulty in developing their strength of character.

In short, the stoic climber knows that, in order to live better, you have to be better, and that implies a set of things that can be tackled through climbing and, at the same time, implemented in all areas of life.

"Waste no more time arguing about what a good man should be. Be one."

Marcus Aurelius[44]

---

[44] Meditations, Book X, 16.

Glossary

AMOR FATI

Latin locution that can be translated as "love of destiny". It is used to describe an attitude in which one sees everything that happens in life as good or, at least, necessary.

ARETÉ

Greek word that can be translated as striving for excellence, for the best version of oneself.

BELAYER

The person who stands below the climbing line and, through the appropriate belay device, handles the climber's rope. He uses his weight to counteract the effects of a climber's fall, thus ensuring the safety of his partner's ascent.

BOLTS

Usually referred to a plate and a bolt that are the metal elements fixedly anchored to the wall along sport climbing routes. Placed every few meters, they allow the climber to place his quickdraws and place the rope through them, preventing a fall beyond the last bolt through which the rope has passed.

BOULDERING

Climbing modality that consists of climbing blocks of rock or small walls, which can be a maximum of eight meters, without the need for conventional climbing protection materials (rope, harness, bolts, etc.), as it is done sideways and reaching a low height.

CHALK BAG

Bag full of magnesium carbonate powder carried by some climbers, is used to remove moisture from the hands and increase grip.

CLIMBING AREA/CRAG

Place that has been set up for the practice of climbing. These are climbing areas where the routes are usually equipped with anchors so that climbing can be done in a fairly safe way, focusing on the sportiest part of climbing.

CLIMBING GRADES

An element of information consisting of assigning values that grade the difficulty of a route. They serve mainly to help us decide if a climb is within our possibilities or not. The most commonly used grade scales in sport climbing are the American and the French scale, but there are many more.

CLIMBING PROJECT

Select a challenging route with the goal of sending it.

Climbing sector

Sectors are areas within a climbing area or crag, composed of a set of routes.

Climbing shoes

Special shoes used for climbing, lightweight and with grippy soles.

Clipping, to clip

Refers to the act of placing the rope through the carabiner of the quickdraw, which will be hanging on a fixed bolt.

Epictetus

Stoic philosopher who lived most of his life as a slave in Rome. After gaining his freedom he devoted himself exclusively to philosophy, even founding his own school. Although he did not write any book, his teachings reach us today thanks to the Enchiridion (Manual) and Discourses, both edited by some of his students.

Fatalism

Belief that all events in the world happen one way and not another according to fate, so they cannot happen any other way and it is better to accept it.

FATE

For some stoics, fate is rather a causal chain of events that result in the things that happen to us in life.

FLASH CLIMBING

Sending a route at the first attempt when you have some information about the route and how to do it. It is different from on-sight climbing.

FREE CLIMBING

Climbing using only one's own skills, without the aid of materials to progress in the ascent. The only equipment used is for protection in case of a fall (such as rope, harness, belays and fixed anchors on the wall).

FREE SOLO

Also called free soloing, it is when the climber climbs walls without the protective equipment (rope, harness, anchors, etc.), forcing himself to rely entirely on their own individual preparation, strength, and skill.

LEAD CLIMBING

Climbing the route passing the rope through the bolts as you ascend. A route is considered sent when it is lead climbed without falling or resting on the anchors.

Marcus Aurelius

Roman emperor between 161 and 180. Nicknamed the Wise or the Philosopher, since besides to governing and participating in military campaigns, he studied philosophy with great dedication. His work *Meditations* is preserved to this day, it was a personal diary that he wrote for himself as a philosophical reflection and was published after his death.

Memento mori

Latin locution that can be translated as "remember that you will die", generally used to reflect on the transience of life. A sort of reminder to make the most of life before it is over.

Oceanic feeling

Sense of eternity, a feeling of being one with the outside world as a whole.

On-Sight climbing

Sending a route without having tried it before or having received information about it.

Premeditatio malorum

Also known as negative visualization, a practice that consists of reflecting on negative future possibilities in order to prevent them, be prepared, or do whatever can be done in the present moment about them.

QUICKDRAW

Two carabiners joined by a sewn sling that are used to attach the rope to the fixed anchors of the route, hooking one carabiner to the plates of the route and passing the climber's rope through the other.

ROUTE

A climbing route is the path a climber uses to climb a wall. Sport climbing routes are usually equipped with fixed anchors that allow the safety rope to be placed along the ascent. They can have different shapes and characteristics and are graded based on their difficulty.

SENDING, TO SEND

Climbing a route (leading) from start to top without falling or using artificial anchors to rest or progress. The anchors and other protection material are only used as a safety measure, but not to facilitate progression.

SENECA

He was one of the Stoic writers whose books have survived to this day. In addition to being a philosopher, he was a Roman statesman, dramatist and writer. He served as Nero's tutor, with a tragic end.

SPORT CLIMBING

Climbing modality understood more as a sport

practice that consists of climbing walls of different difficulties equipped with fixed anchors placed to protect the climber's safety.

STOICISM

Philosophical school founded in Athens by Zeno of Citium in 301 B.C. It focuses its doctrine on the search for happiness through the control of the emotions that disturb life.

TOP ROPE CLIMBING

Climbing with the rope already mounted on a top anchor so that the rope is always above the climber. It is the safest way, ideal for beginners.

VIRTUE

Desirable characteristics for proceeding in accordance with certain ideals. In the concept of Stoic virtue, serenity and strength of character were especially valued as keys to leading a good, virtuous life.

Stoic readings

RECOMMENDED READINGS

Classical Stoicism
Marcus Aurelius, *Meditations*
Seneca, *De Tranquillitate Animi (On the tranquillity of mind)*
—, De *Brevitate Vitæ (On the shortness of life)*
—, De *Vita Beata (On the Happy Life)*
—, De *Ira (On anger)*
—, *Epistulae morales ad Lucilium (Moral letters to Lucilius)*
Epictetus, Enchiridion (by Arrian)

Contemporary Stoicism

Holiday, R. (2015): The obstacle is the way. Profile Books
Irvine, W. (2009): A Guide to the Good Life. Oxford University Press

BIBLIOGRAPHY

Aurelius, M., & Hays, G. (2003). Meditations: A new translation. Random House
Aurelius, M., & Bach, R. (1977). Meditaciones. Gredos
Aurelius, M., & Pierre Hadot. (1998) Marc Aurèle. Ecrits pour lui même. Belles Lettres
Aurelius, M., & Farquharson, A. (1992). Meditations. Every man's Library
Epicteto & Ortiz, P. (1993). Disertaciones. Gredos
Epicteto & Mosquera, M (2003) Manual de Epicteto. Biblioteca Nueva Era
Epicteto & Dobbin, R. (2008). Discourses and selected writings. Penguin UK
Seneca, L. A & Gummere, R (1920). Moral Letters to Lucilius
Seneca, L. A & Clode, W. (1888). The Morals of Seneca. A selection of his prose
Seneca, L. A & Basore, J. (1932). On the shortness of life
Seneca, L. A., & Campbell, R. (1969). Letters from a Stoic. Penguin Classics

Subscribe to keep finding wisdom on
the rock with us!

climbingletters.com/mail

Printed in Great Britain
by Amazon